WALDEN

Henry David Thoreau

TECHNICAL DIRECTOR Maxwell Krohn
EDITORIAL DIRECTOR Justin Kestler
MANAGING EDITOR Ben Florman

SERIES EDITORS Boomie Aglietti, Justin Kestler
PRODUCTION Christian Lorentzen

WRITERS Amanda Davis, Jim Cocola, John Henriksen
EDITORS Jesse Hawkes, John Crowther

This edition published by Spark Publishing

Spark Publishing
A Division of SparkNotes LLC
120 Fifth Avenue, 8th Floor
New York, NY 10011

02 03 04 05 SN 9 8 7 6 5 4 3 2 1

Please send all comments and questions or report errors to
feedback@sparknotes.com.

Library of Congress information available upon request

Printed and bound in the United States

RRD-C

ISBN 1-58663-445-3

INTRODUCTION:
STOPPING TO
BUY SPARKNOTES
ON A
SNOWY EVENING

Whose words these are you *think* you know.
Your paper's due tomorrow, though;
We're glad to see you stopping here
To get some help before you go.

Lost your course? You'll find it here.
Face tests and essays without fear.
Between the words, good grades at stake:
Get great results throughout the year.

Once school bells caused your heart to quake
As teachers circled each mistake.
Use SparkNotes and no longer weep,
Ace every single test you take.

Yes, books are lovely, dark, and deep,
But only what you grasp you keep,
With hours to go before you sleep,
With hours to go before you sleep.

CONTENTS

CONTEXT

H ENRY DAVID THOREAU WAS BORN in Concord, Massachusetts on July 12, 1817, the third child of John Thoreau and Cynthia Dunbar Thoreau. The freethinking Thoreaus were relatively cultured, but they were also poor, making their living by the modest production of homemade pencils. Despite financial constraints, Henry received a top-notch education, first at Concord Academy and then at Harvard College in nearby Cambridge, Massachusetts. His education there included ancient and modern European languages and literatures, philosophy, theology, and history. Graduating from Harvard in 1837, Thoreau returned to Concord to teach in the local grammar school, but resigned abruptly in only his second week on the job, declaring himself unable to inflict corporal punishment on misbehaving pupils. In the ensuing months, Thoreau sought another teaching job unsuccessfully. It was around this time that Thoreau met Ralph Waldo Emerson, a prominent American philosopher, essayist, and poet who had recently moved to Concord. The friendship between the two would eventually prove the most influential of Thoreau's life. The following June, Thoreau founded a small progressive school emphasizing intellectual curiosity over rote memorization, and after a period of success for the school, his brother John joined the venture. After several years, John's failing health and Henry's impatience for larger projects made it impossible to continue running the school.

During this period, Thoreau assisted his family in pencil manufacturing, and worked for a time as a town surveyor. He also began to keep an extensive journal, to which he would devote considerable energy over the next twenty-five years. His writing activities deepened as his friendship with Emerson developed and as he was exposed to the Transcendentalist movement, of which Emerson was the figurehead. Transcendentalism drew heavily on the idealist and otherworldly aspects of English and German Romanticism, Hindu and Buddhist thought, and the tenets of Confucius and Mencius. It emphasized the individual heart, mind, and soul as the center of the universe and made objective facts secondary to personal truth. It construed self-reliance, as expounded in Emerson's famous 1841 essay by that same title, not just as an economic virtue but also as a whole philosophical and spiritual basis for existence. And, importantly for Thoreau, it sanctioned a disavowal or rejection of any social norms, traditions, or values that contradict one's own personal vision.

With his unorthodox manners and irreverent views, Thoreau quickly made a name for himself among Emerson's followers, who encouraged him to publish essays in *The Dial*, an emerging Transcendentalist magazine established by Margaret Fuller. Among these early works were the first of Thoreau's nature writings, along with a number of poems and a handful of book reviews. Thoreau began to enjoy modest success as a writer. His personal life was marred by his rejected marriage proposal to Ellen Sewall in 1840, who was forced to turn down Thoreau (as she had turned down his brother, John, before him) because of pressure from her family, who considered the Thoreaus to be financially unstable and suspiciously radical. Disappointed in love, devastated by the 1842 death of his brother, and unable to secure literary work in New York, Thoreau was soon back in Concord, once again pressed into service in the family pencil business.

During the early 1840s, Thoreau lived as a pensioner at the Emerson address, where he helped maintain the house and garden, and provided companionship to Emerson's second wife, Lidian. Thoreau and Lidian developed an intimate, but wholly platonic friendship. It was on Emerson's land at Walden Pond that Thoreau, inspired by the experiment of his Harvard classmate, Charles Stearns Wheeler, erected a small dwelling in which to live closer to nature. On July 4, 1845, his cabin complete, Thoreau moved to the woods by Walden Pond. He spent the next two years there composing the initial drafts to the two works on which his later reputation would largely rest: *A Week on the Concord and Merrimack Rivers,* first published in 1849, and *Walden; or, Life in the Woods,* first published in 1854. Thoreau's isolation during this period is sometimes exaggerated. He lived within easy walking distance of Concord, and received frequent visitors in his shack, most often his close friend and traveling companion William Ellery Channing.

During a journey Thoreau made to Concord in July of 1846, the constable apprehended and imprisoned him for nonpayment of a poll tax that he refused to pay because it supported a nation endorsing slavery. In the mild scandal aroused by this gesture against authority, Thoreau defended his actions in a lecture to the Concord Lyceum, in which he publicly expounded his reasons for resisting state authority. Later he revised and published this lecture under the title "Civil Disobedience," which is the most internationally known of Thoreau's works, inspiring such prominent social thinkers as Leo Tolstoy and Mahatma Gandhi.

When Emerson went to Europe for an extended stay in the autumn of 1847, Thoreau left Walden to keep house with Lidian again for nearly two years. After Emerson's return, tensions between the two men caused a rift in their friendship. Thoreau left the Emerson residence and returned to his family home, where he would remain for the rest of his life, and resumed work in the pencil business. As the slavery debate came to a head in the 1850s, Thoreau took on a vocal role in the burgeoning abolitionist movement. He assisted fugitive slaves on the Underground Railroad, and later took an unpopular stand by announcing his support for the martyred John Brown, who in 1859 had sought to incite a slave rebellion in Harper's Ferry, Virginia. But during a protracted bout of tuberculosis in the late 1850s, Thoreau largely retreated from public concerns. He began a study of growth rings in forest trees, and visited Minnesota on a walking tour in the spring of 1861. But his illness finally overcame him, and he died at home in Concord on May 6, 1862, at the age of forty-four.

Although Thoreau is held today in great esteem, his work received far less attention during his lifetime, and a considerable number of his neighbors viewed him with contempt. As a result, Thoreau had to self-finance the publication of his first book, *A Week on the Concord and Merrimack Rivers.* Published in an edition of 1,000, over 700 of these copies remained unsold, and he eventually stored them on his home bookshelves; Thoreau liked to joke that he had written an entire library. Even *Walden* was met with scant interest. He revised the work eight times before a publisher accepted it, and the book found only marginal success during Thoreau's lifetime. It was not until the twentieth century that Thoreau's extraordinary impact on American culture would be felt. In the upsurge in counterculture sentiment during the Vietnam War and the Civil Rights era, *Walden* and "Civil Disobedience" inspired many young Americans to express their disavowal of official U.S. policies and declare ideological independence, even at the risk of arrest. *Walden* also expressed a critique of consumerism and capitalism that was congenial to the hippies and others who preferred to drop out of the bustle of consumer society and pursue what they saw as greater and more personally meaningful aims. Moreover,

CONTEXT

Thoreau politicized the American landscape and nature itself, giving us a liberal view on the wilderness whose legacy can be felt in the Sierra Club and the Green Party. He did not perceive nature as a dead and passive object of conquest and exploitation, as it was for many of the early pioneers for whom land meant survival. Rather, he saw in it a lively and vibrant world unto itself, a spectacle of change, growth, and constancy that could infuse us all with spiritual meaning if we pursued it. Finally, Thoreau gave generations of American writers a distinctive style to emulate: a combination of homey, folksy talk with erudite allusions, creating a tone that is both casual and majestic.

PLOT OVERVIEW

WALDEN opens with a simple announcement that Thoreau spent two years in Walden Pond, near Concord, Massachusetts, living a simple life supported by no one. He says that he now resides among the civilized again; the episode was clearly both experimental and temporary. The first chapter, "Economy," is a manifesto of social thought and meditations on domestic management, and in it Thoreau sketches out his ideals as he describes his pond project. He devotes attention to the skepticism and wonderment with which townspeople had greeted news of his project, and he defends himself from their views that society is the only place to live. He recounts the circumstances of his move to Walden Pond, along with a detailed account of the steps he took to construct his rustic habitation and the methods by which he supported himself in the course of his wilderness experiment. It is a chapter full of facts, figures, and practical advice, but also offers big ideas about the claims of individualism versus social existence, all interspersed with evidence of scholarship and a propensity for humor.

Thoreau tells us that he completed his cabin in the spring of 1845 and moved in on July 4 of that year. Most of the materials and tools he used to build his home he borrowed or scrounged from previous sites. The land he squats on belongs to his friend Ralph Waldo Emerson; he details a cost-analysis of the entire construction project. In order to make a little money, Thoreau cultivates a modest bean-field, a job that tends to occupy his mornings. He reserves his afternoons and evenings for contemplation, reading, and walking about the countryside. Endorsing the values of austerity, simplicity, and solitude, Thoreau consistently emphasizes the minimalism of his lifestyle and the contentment to be derived from it. He repeatedly contrasts his own freedom with the imprisonment of others who devote their lives to material prosperity.

Despite his isolation, Thoreau feels the presence of society surrounding him. The Fitchburg Railroad rushes past Walden Pond, interrupting his reveries and forcing him to contemplate the power of technology. Thoreau also finds occasion to converse with a wide range of other people, such as the occasional peasant farmer, railroad worker, or the odd visitor to Walden. He describes in some

5

detail his association with a Canadian-born woodcutter, Alex Therien, who is grand and sincere in his character, though modest in intellectual attainments. Thoreau makes frequent trips into Concord to seek the society of his longtime friends and to conduct what scattered business the season demands. On one such trip, Thoreau spends a night in jail for refusing to pay a poll tax because, he says, the government supports slavery. Released the next day, Thoreau returns to Walden.

Thoreau devotes great attention to nature, the passing of the seasons, and the creatures with which he shares the woods. He recounts the habits of a panoply of animals, from woodchucks to partridges. Some he endows with a larger meaning, often spiritual or psychological. The hooting loon that plays hide and seek with Thoreau, for instance, becomes a symbol of the playfulness of nature and its divine laughter at human endeavors. Another example of animal symbolism is the full-fledged ant war that Thoreau stumbles upon, prompting him to meditate on human warfare. Thoreau's interest in animals is not exactly like the naturalist's or zoologist's. He does not observe and describe them neutrally and scientifically, but gives them a moral and philosophical significance, as if each has a distinctive lesson to teach him.

As autumn turns to winter, Thoreau begins preparations for the arrival of the cold. He listens to the squirrel, the rabbit, and the fox as they scuttle about gathering food. He watches the migrating birds, and welcomes the pests that infest his cabin as they escape the coming frosts. He prepares his walls with plaster to shut out the wind. By day he makes a study of the snow and ice, giving special attention to the mystic blue ice of Walden Pond, and by night he sits and listens to the wind as it whips and whistles outside his door. Thoreau occasionally sees ice-fishermen come to cut out huge blocks that are shipped off to cities, and contemplates how most of the ice will melt and flow back to Walden Pond. Occasionally Thoreau receives a visit from a friend like William Ellery Channing or Amos Bronson Alcott, but for the most part he is alone. In one chapter, he conjures up visions of earlier residents of Walden Pond long dead and largely forgotten, including poor tradesmen and former slaves. Thoreau prefers to see himself in their company, rather than amid the cultivated and wealthy classes.

As he becomes acquainted with Walden Pond and neighboring ponds, Thoreau wants to map their layout and measure their depths. Thoreau finds that Walden Pond is no more than a hundred feet deep, thereby refuting common folk wisdom that it is bottom-less. He meditates on the pond as a symbol of infinity that people need in their lives. Eventually winter gives way to spring, and with a huge crash and roar the ice of Walden Pond begins to melt and hit the shore. In lyric imagery echoing the onset of Judgment Day, Thoreau describes the coming of spring as a vast transformation of the face of the world, a time when all sins are forgiven.

Thoreau announces that his project at the pond is over, and that he returned to civilized life on September 6, 1847. The revitalization of the landscape suggests the restoration of the full powers of the human soul, and Thoreau's narrative observations give way, in the last chapter of *Walden*, to a more direct sermonizing about the untapped potential within humanity. In visionary language, Thoreau exhorts us to "meet" our lives and live fully.

CHARACTER LIST

There are no major characters in Walden *other than Thoreau, who is both the narrator and the main human subject of his narrative. The following list identifies figures who appear in the work, as well as historical figures to whom Thoreau refers.*

Henry David Thoreau Amateur naturalist, essayist, lover of solitude, and poet. Thoreau was a student and protégé of the great American philosopher and essayist Ralph Waldo Emerson, and his construction of a hut on Emerson's land at Walden Pond is a fitting symbol of the intellectual debt that Thoreau owed to Emerson. Strongly influenced by Transcendentalism, Thoreau believed in the perfectibility of mankind through education, self-exploration, and spiritual awareness. This view dominates almost all of Thoreau's writing, even the most mundane and trivial, so that even woodchucks and ants take on allegorical meaning. A former teacher, Thoreau's didactic impulse transforms a work that begins as economic reflection and nature writing to something that ends far more like a sermon. Although he values poverty theoretically, he seems a bit of a snob when talking with actual poor people. His style underscores this point, since his writing is full of classical references and snippets of poetry that the educated would grasp but the underprivileged would not.

Ralph Waldo Emerson Essayist, poet, and the leading figure of Transcendentalism. Emerson became a mentor to Thoreau after they met in 1837. Emerson played a significant role in the creation of *Walden* by allowing Thoreau to live and build on his property near Walden Pond. There is an appropriate symbolism in this construction site, since philosophically Thoreau was building on the Transcendentalist foundation already prepared by Emerson. The influence of Emerson's ideas, especially the doctrine of self-reliance that sees

9

the human soul and mind as the origin of the reality it inhabits, pervades Thoreau's work. However, whereas Thoreau retreated to his own private world, Emerson assumed a prominent role in public life, making extended overseas lecture tours to promote the view expressed in his renowned *Essays*. The two often disagreed on the necessity of adhering to some public conventions, and the heated tensions between the two may perhaps be felt in the minimal attention Emerson receives in *Walden*. Thoreau utterly fails to mention that Emerson owns the land, despite his tedious detailing of less significant facts, and when Emerson visits, in the guise of the unnamed "Old Immortal," Thoreau treats him rather indifferently.

Alex Therien A laborer in his late twenties who often works in the vicinity of Thoreau's abode. Thoreau describes Therien as "a Canadian, a wood-chopper and post-maker," asserting that it would be difficult to find a more simple or natural human being. Although he is not a reader, Therien is nevertheless conversant and intelligent, and thus he holds great appeal for Thoreau as a sort of untutored backwoods sage. Thoreau compares the woodcutter to Walden Pond itself, saying both possess hidden depths.

John Field A poor Irish-American laborer who lives with his wife and children on the Baker Farm just outside of Concord. Thoreau uses Field as an example of an "honest, hard-working, but shiftless man," someone who is forced to struggle at a great disadvantage in life because he lacks unusual natural abilities or social position. The conversation that Thoreau and Field have when Thoreau runs to the Field home for shelter in a rainstorm is an uncomfortable reminder that Thoreau's ideas and convictions may set him apart from those same poor people that he elsewhere idealizes. Rather than converse casually with Field, Thoreau gives him a heated lecture on the merits of cutting down on coffee and meat consumption. Overall, his treatment of Field seems condescending.

His parting regret that Field suffers from an "inherited" Irish proclivity to laziness casts a strangely ungenerous, even slightly racist light over all of Thoreau's ideas.

Amos Bronson Alcott A friend whom Thoreau refers to as "the philosopher." Alcott was a noted educator and social reformer, as well as the father of beloved children's author Louisa May Alcott. In 1834 he founded the Temple School in Boston, a noted progressive school that spawned many imitators. Affiliated with the Transcendentalists, he was known for a set of aphorisms titled "Orphic Sayings" that appeared in *The Dial*. Alcott also had a hand in the utopian communities of Brook Farm and Fruitlands, and went on to become the superintendent of the Concord public schools.

William Ellery Channing Thoreau's closest friend, an amateur poet and an affiliate of the Transcendentalists. Channing was named after his uncle, a noted Unitarian clergyman. His son, Edward Channing, went on to become a noted professor of history at Harvard University.

Henry Clay A prominent Whig senator from Kentucky. Clay ran unsuccessfully for president on three occasions. He was a supporter of internal improvements as a part of his American System, and is well known as "the Great Compromiser" for his role in the Missouri Compromise and the Compromise of 1850. Thoreau was a staunch critic of Clay and of the expansionism that Clay advocated.

Lidian Emerson Emerson's second wife. Lidian Emerson was somewhat distressed by her husband's frequent absences from home. During her husband's tours of Europe, Thoreau stayed with her, and the two developed a close friendship.

Confucius A Chinese sage of the sixth century B.C., known for his sayings and parables collected under the title *Analects*. His teachings gave rise to a sort of secular religion known as Confucianism, which served as a model for the Chinese government in subsequent centuries. Confucius also had a significant effect on the Transcendentalist movement, and was one of Thoreau's favorite authors.

James Russell Lowell A Harvard-trained lawyer. Lowell eventually abandoned his first vocation for a career in letters. His poetic satire *The Bigelow Papers* was well received, and he went on to become a professor of modern languages at Harvard and the first editor of the *Atlantic Monthly*.

Mencius A Chinese sage of the fourth century B.C. and a disciple of Confucius. Mencius was best known for his anthology of sayings and stories collected under the title *The Book of Mencius,* and did much to promote the reputation of Confucius, although he himself was not widely venerated until more than a thousand years later. Like his master's work, Mencius's combination of respect for social harmony and the inward reconciliation with the universe exerted a powerful influence on Thoreau.

John Thoreau Elder brother to Henry David Thoreau. The two brothers oversaw and taught at the Concord Academy, a progressive independent school, from 1838 to 1841. John Thoreau's failing health was a contributing factor in the demise of the school, and he died in 1842 from complications related to lockjaw.

ANALYSIS OF MAJOR CHARACTERS

HENRY DAVID THOREAU

As the foremost American proponent of simple living, Thoreau remains a powerful influence on generation after generation of young freethinkers, but his political importance is more complex than is often thought. It is the liberal side of Thoreau that is most widely remembered today. He sought an absolutely individual stance toward everything, looking for the truth not in social conventions or inherited traditions but only in himself. His casual determination to say "no" to anything he did not care for, or stand for, affirmed and solidified the American model of conscientious objection, a model that resurfaced most notably during the Vietnam War era. His skepticism toward American consumer culture, still in its infancy in the mid-nineteenth century, is even more applicable today than it was in 1847. His willingness to downgrade his lifestyle in return for the satisfactions of self-reliance has set a standard for independent young people for more than a century and a half. It could be argued that Thoreau had significant influence on the profile of American liberalism and of American counterculture.

But Thoreau has a half-hidden conservative side. This schism has led him, paradoxically, to be viewed as godfather of both the hippie movement and anti-technology, rural conservatives. His harsh view of the Fitchburg Railway (as he expresses it in the chapter "Sounds") makes modern transportation innovations seem not a boon to his society, but rather a demonic force that threatens natural harmony. His eulogy of a humble lifestyle does not lead him to solidarity with the working poor or to any sort of community-based feeling; rather, it makes him a bit isolated, strangely distant from his neighbors. Thoreau consistently criticizes neighbors he considers bestial, although he theoretically endorses their simplicity. He praises the grand woodchopper Alex Therien, for example, only to abruptly dismiss Therien as being too uncouth, too immersed in "animal nature." The unfairness of this dismissal leaves a bitter taste in our mouths, making us wonder whether Thoreau would quietly reject other poor workers as excessively animal-like. Similarly, his preachy and rather condescending lecture toward the humble Field family, in whose house he seeks shelter from a rainstorm, shows no signs of any desire to make contact with the poor on an equal footing with himself. He may want to be their instructor and guide, but not really their friend or comrade. Most damning is Thoreau's unpleasant, almost racist remark that the Fields' poverty is an "inherited" Irish trait, as if implying that non-Anglo immigrants are genetically incapable of the noble frugality and resourcefulness that distinguishes Thoreau.

Thoreau's literary style is often overshadowed by his political and ideological significance, but it is equally important, and just as innovative and free as his social thought. He is a subtle punster and ironist, as when he describes the sun as "too warm a friend," or when he calls the ability to weave men's trousers a "virtue" (a play on the Latin word *vir,* which means "man"). He uses poetic devices, such as personification, not in a grandiose poetic manner, but in a casual and easygoing one: when he drags his desk and chair out for housecleaning, he describes them as being happy outdoors and reluctant to go back inside. His richly allusive style is brilliantly combined with a down-home feel, so that Thoreau moves from quoting Confucius to talking about woodchucks without a jolt. This combination of the everyday and the erudite finds echoes in later writers such as E. B. White, who also used a rural setting for his witty meditations on life and human nature. Moreover, we feel that Thoreau is not an armchair reader of literary classics, but is rather attempting to use his erudition to enrich the life he lives in a practical spirit, as when he describes Alex Therien as "Homeric" right after quoting a passage from Homer's work. Homer is not just an old dead poet to Thoreau, but rather a way of seeing the world around him. Thoreau's style is lyrical in places, allegorical in others, and sometimes both at once, as when the poetic beauty of the "Ponds" chapter becomes a delicate allegory for the purity of the human soul. He is a private and ruminative writer rather than a social one, which explains the almost total absence of dialogue in his writing. Yet his writing has an imposing sense of social purpose, and we are aware that despite his claimed yearning for privacy, Thoreau hungers for a large audience to hear his words. The final chapters of *Walden* almost cease being nature writing, and become a straightforward sermon. A private thinker, Thoreau is also a public preacher, whether or not he admits it.

ALEX THERIEN

Thoreau's occasional visitor, Therien is the individual in the work who comes closest to being considered a friend, although there is always a distance between the two that reveals much about Thoreau's prejudices. The hermit and the woodsman are both contented with a humble backwoods life; both take a pleasure in physical exertion (Therien is a woodchopper and post-driver, Thoreau is a bean-cultivator); and both are of French Canadian descent, as their names indicate. Thoreau describes Therien as "Homeric" in Chapter 6, voicing a deep tribute to a naturally noble man who is as heroic in his sheer vitality as Odysseus or Achilles, the heroes of Homer's two epic poems, despite the man's lack of formal education and social polish. Therien seems remote from social customs, as when he happily dines on a woodchuck caught by his dog. Nevertheless, he strikes people as inwardly aristocratic ("a prince in disguise," according to one townsman). He is sensitive to great art, as when Thoreau reads a passage from Homer's *Iliad* to him, and Therien responds with the simple and resounding praise, "That's good." He may not fully grasp what he has heard, but he can appreciate the beauty of it nonetheless. He shows a powerful moral sense, as when he spends his Sunday morning gathering white oak bark for a sick man, not complaining about the task. Therien is an astonishing worker to an almost mythical degree, capable of driving fifty posts in a day, and claiming that he has never been tired in his life. Yet he is also artistic in his labor, and can think of nothing more pleasurable than tree chopping.

In all these qualities, Therien seems Thoreau's ideal man. Therien does not "play any part" or perform any fake social role, but is always only himself, as true to himself as Thoreau elsewhere says he aims to be. Therien is absolutely "genuine and unsophisticated," and is "simply and naturally humble." Thoreau is not sure whether Therien is as wise as Shakespeare or as ignorant as a child, thus indirectly acknowledging that the man is both, displaying a kind of wise ignorance. Thoreau suspects that Therien is a man of genius, as profound as Walden Pond, despite his muddy surface. We feel how closely identified Therien is with Thoreau's own self-image: a wisely ignorant, hard-working, independent genius of the backwoods.

Strikingly, Thoreau never describes Therien as his friend, but always merely as a man who visits him, leaving a gulf between the two men. This unbridgeable divide is basically rooted in their differing levels of education. Therien is not a reader, and is "so deeply immersed in his animal life" that he can never carry on the kind of higher conversation Thoreau values. Thoreau mentions this flaw in Therien at the end of the passage describing him, and it feels like a kind of mild damnation, since Therien never appears again in *Walden*. The label "animal" also feels a bit unfair, as we may wonder what exactly separates Thoreau from the animal-like Therien and other beasts. A taste for reading alone surely does not make all the difference. It may be that Thoreau simply cannot imagine any rival for his role as natural genius, and must downgrade Therien before dismissing him. The relationship with Therien may make us wonder whether Thoreau's individualism is—at least sometimes—a bit ungenerous, self-centered, and proud.

THEMES, MOTIFS & SYMBOLS

THEMES

Themes are the fundamental and often universal ideas explored in a literary work.

THE IMPORTANCE OF SELF-RELIANCE

Four years before Thoreau embarked on his Walden project, his great teacher and role model Ralph Waldo Emerson wrote an enormously influential essay entitled "Self-Reliance." It can be seen as a statement of the philosophical ideals that Thoreau's experiment is meant to put into practice. Certainly self-reliance is economic and social in *Walden Pond*: it is the principle that in matters of financial and interpersonal relations, independence is more valuable than neediness. Thus Thoreau dwells on the contentment of his solitude, on his finding entertainment in the laugh of the loon and the march of the ants rather than in balls, marketplaces, or salons. He does not disdain human companionship; in fact he values it highly when it comes on his own terms, as when his philosopher or poet friends come to call. He simply refuses to need human society. Similarly, in economic affairs he is almost obsessed with the idea that he can support himself through his own labor, producing more than he consumes, and working to produce a profit. Thoreau does not simply report on the results of his accounting, but gives us a detailed list of expenditures and income. How much money he spent on salt from 1845 to 1847 may seem trivial, but for him it is not. Rather it is proof that, when everything is added up, he is a giver rather than a taker in the economic game of life.

As Emerson's essay details, self-reliance can be spiritual as well as economic, and Thoreau follows Emerson in exploring the higher dimensions of individualism. In Transcendentalist thought the self is the absolute center of reality; everything external is an emanation of the self that takes its reality from our inner selves. Self-reliance thus refers not just to paying one's own bills, but also more philosophically to the way the natural world and humankind rely on the self to exist. This duality explains the connection between Thoreau the accountant and Thoreau the poet, and shows why the man who is so interested in pinching pennies is the same man who exults lyrically over a partridge or a winter sky. They are both products of self-reliance, since the economizing that allows Thoreau to live on Walden Pond also allows him to feel one with nature, to feel as though it is part of his own soul.

THE VALUE OF SIMPLICITY

Simplicity is more than a mode of life for Thoreau; it is a philosophical ideal as well. In his "Economy" chapter, Thoreau asserts that a feeling of dissatisfaction with one's possessions can be resolved in two ways: one may acquire more, or reduce one's desires. Thoreau looks around at his fellow Concord residents and finds them taking the first path, devoting their energies to making mortgage payments and buying the latest fashions. He prefers to take the second path of radically minimizing his consumer activity. Thoreau patches his clothes instead of buying new ones and dispenses with all accessories he finds unnecessary. For Thoreau, anything more than what is useful is not just an extravagance, but a real impediment and disadvantage. He builds his own shack instead of getting a bank loan to buy one, and enjoys the leisure time that he can afford by renouncing larger expenditures. Ironically, he points out, those who pursue more impressive possessions actually have fewer possessions than he does, since he owns his house outright, while theirs are technically held by mortgage companies. He argues that the simplification of one's lifestyle does not hinder such pleasures as owning one's residence, but on the contrary, facilitates them.

Another irony of Thoreau's simplification campaign is that his literary style, while concise, is far from simple. It contains witticisms, double meanings, and puns that are not at all the kind of New England deadpan literalism that might pass for literary simplicity. Despite its minimalist message, *Walden* is an elevated text that would have been much more accessible to educated city-dwellers than to the predominantly uneducated country-dwellers.

THE ILLUSION OF PROGRESS

Living in a culture fascinated by the idea of progress represented by technological, economic, and territorial advances, Thoreau is stubbornly skeptical of the idea that any outward improvement of life can bring the inner peace and contentment he craves. In an era of enormous capitalist expansion, Thoreau is doggedly anti-consumption, and in a time of pioneer migrations he lauds the pleasures of staying put. In a century notorious for its smugness toward all that preceded it, Thoreau points out the stifling conventionality and constraining labor conditions that made nineteenth-century progress possible.

One clear illustration of Thoreau's resistance to progress is his criticism of the train, which throughout Europe and America was a symbol of the wonders and advantages of technological progress. Although he enjoys imagining the local Fitchburg train as a mythical roaring beast in the chapter entitled "Sounds," he generally seems peeved by the encroachment of the railway upon the rustic calm of Walden Pond. Like Tolstoy in Russia, Thoreau in the United States dissents from his society's enthusiasm for this innovation in transportation, seeing it rather as a false idol of social progress. It moves people from one point to another faster, but Thoreau has little use for travel anyway, asking the reason for going off "to count the cats in Zanzibar." It is far better for him to go vegetate in a little corner of the woods for two years than to commute from place to place unreflectively.

Thoreau is skeptical, as well, of the change in popular mindset brought by train travel. "Have not men improved somewhat in punctuality since the railroad was invented?" he asks with scarcely concealed irony, as if punctuality were the greatest virtue progress can offer. People "talk and think faster in the depot" than they did earlier in stagecoach offices, but here again, speedy talk and quick thinking are hardly preferable to thoughtful speech and deep thinking. Trains, like all technological "improvements" give people an illusion of heightened freedom, but in fact represent a new servitude, since one must always be subservient to fixed train schedules and routes. For Thoreau, the train has given us a new illusion of a controlling destiny: "We have constructed a fate, a new *Atropos*, that never turns aside." As the Greek goddess Atropos worked—she determined the length of human lives and could never be swayed (her name means "unswerving")—so too does the train chug along on its fixed path and make us believe that our lives must too.

MOTIFS

Motifs are recurring structures, contrasts, or literary devices that can help to develop and inform the text's major themes.

THE SEASONAL CYCLE

The narrative of *Walden*, which at first seems haphazard and unplanned, is actually quite consciously put together to mirror the cycle of the seasons. The compression of Thoreau's two actual years (1845 to 1847) into one narrative year shows how relatively unimportant the documentary or logbook aspect of his writing is. He cares less for the real calendar time taken up by his project than for the symbolic time he projects onto it. One full year, from springtime to springtime, echoes the Christian idea of rebirth, moving from one beginning to a new one. (We can imagine how very different *Walden* might be if it went from December to December, for example.) Thus each season inevitably carries with it not just its usual calendar attributes, but a spiritual resonance as well. The story begins in the spring of 1845, as Thoreau begins construction on his cabin. He moves in, fittingly and probably quite intentionally, on Independence Day, July 4—making his symbolic declaration of independence from society, and drawing closer to the true sources of his being. The summer is a time of physical activity, as he narrates in great detail his various construction projects and domestic management solutions. He also begins his cultivation of the bean-fields, following the natural cycle of the seasons like any farmer, but also echoing the biblical phrase from Ecclesiastes, "a time to reap, a time to sow." It may be more than the actual beans he harvests, and his produce may be for the soul as well as for the marketplace. Winter is a time of reflection and inwardness, as he mostly communes with himself indoors and has only a few choice visitors. It is in winter that he undertakes the measuring of the pond, which becomes a symbol of plumbing his own spiritual depths in solitude. Then in spring come echoes of Judgment Day, with the crash of melting ice and the trumpeting of the geese; Thoreau feels all sins forgiven. The cycle of seasons is thus a cycle of moral and spiritual regeneration made possible by a communion with nature and with oneself.

POETRY

The moral directness and hardheaded practical bookkeeping matters with which Thoreau inaugurates *Walden* do not prepare us for the lyrical outbursts that occur quite frequently and regularly in the work. Factual and detail-minded, Thoreau is capable of some extraordinary imaginary visions, which he intersperses within economic matters in a highly unexpected way. In his chapter "The Bean-Field," for example, Thoreau tells us that he spent fifty-four cents on a hoe, and then soon after quotes a verse about wings spreading and closing in preparation for flight. The down-to-earth hoe and the winged flight of fancy are closely juxtaposed in a way typical of the whole work.

Occasionally the lyricism is a quotation of other people's poems, as when Thoreau quotes a Homeric epic in introducing the noble figure of Alex Therien. At other times, as in the beautiful "Ponds" chapter, Thoreau allows his prose to become lyrical, as when he describes the mystical blue ice of Walden Pond. The intermittent lyricism of *Walden* is more than just a pleasant decorative addition or stylistic curiosity. It delivers the powerful philosophical message that there is higher meaning and transcendent value in even the most humble stay in a simple hut by a pond. Hoeing beans, which some might consider the antithesis of poetry, is actually a deeply lyrical and meaningful experience when seen in the right way.

MOTIFS

Imaginary People

Thoreau mentions several actual people in *Walden,* but curiously, he also devotes considerable attention to describing nonexistent or imaginary people. At the beginning of the chapter "Former Inhabitants," Thoreau frankly acknowledges that in his winter isolation he was forced to invent imaginary company for himself. This conjuring is the work of his imagination, but it is also historically accurate, since the people he conjures are based on memories of old-timers who remember earlier neighbors now long gone. Thoreau's imaginary companions are thus somewhere between fact and fiction, reality and fantasy. When Thoreau describes these former inhabitants in vivid detail, we can easily forget that they are now dead: they seem too real.

Thoreau also manages to make *actual* people seem imaginary. He never uses proper names when referring to friends and associates in *Walden,* rendering them mythical. After Thoreau describes Alex Therien as a Homeric hero, we cannot help seeing him in a somewhat poetic and unreal way, despite all the realism of Thoreau's introduction. He doesn't name even his great spiritual teacher, Emerson, but obliquely calls him the "Old Immortal." The culmination of this continual transformation of people into myths or ideas is Thoreau's expectation of "the Visitor who never comes," which he borrows from the Vedas, a Hindu sacred text. This remark lets us see how spiritual all of Thoreau's imaginary people are. The real person, for him, is not the villager with a name, but rather the transcendent soul behind that external social persona.

SYMBOLS

Symbols are objects, characters, figures, or colors used to represent abstract ideas or concepts.

WALDEN POND

The meanings of Walden Pond are various, and by the end of the work this small body of water comes to symbolize almost everything Thoreau holds dear spiritually, philosophically, and personally. Certainly it symbolizes the alternative to, and withdrawal from, social conventions and obligations. But it also symbolizes the vitality and tranquility of nature. A clue to the symbolic meaning of the pond lies in two of its aspects that fascinate Thoreau: its depth, rumored to be infinite, and its pure and reflective quality. Thoreau is so intrigued by the question of how deep Walden Pond is that he devises a new method of plumbing depths to measure it himself, finding it no more than a hundred feet deep. Wondering why people rumor that the pond is bottomless, Thoreau offers a spiritual explanation: humans need to believe in infinity. He suggests that the pond is not just a natural phenomenon, but also a metaphor for spiritual belief. When he later describes the pond reflecting heaven and making the swimmer's body pure white, we feel that Thoreau too is turning the water (as in the Christian sacrament of baptism by holy water) into a symbol of heavenly purity available to humankind on earth. When Thoreau concludes his chapter on "The Ponds" with the memorable line, "Talk of heaven! ye disgrace earth," we see him unwilling to subordinate earth to heaven. Thoreau finds heaven within himself, and it is symbolized by the pond, "looking into which the beholder measures the depth of his own nature." By the end of the "Ponds" chapter, the water hardly seems like a physical part of the external landscape at all anymore; it has become one with the heavenly soul of humankind.

ANIMALS

As Thoreau's chief companions after he moves to Walden Pond, animals inevitably symbolize his retreat from human society and closer intimacy with the natural world. Thoreau devotes much attention in his narrative to the behavior patterns of woodchucks, partridges, loons, and mice, among others. Yet his animal writing does not sound like the notes of a naturalist; there is nothing truly scientific or zoological in *Walden,* for Thoreau personalizes nature too much. He does not record animals neutrally, but instead emphasizes their human characteristics, turning them into short vignettes of human behavior somewhat in the fashion of Aesop's fables. For example, Thoreau's observation of the partridge and its young walking along his windowsill elicits a meditation on motherhood and the maternal urge to protect one's offspring. Similarly, when Thoreau watches two armies of ants wage war with all the "ferocity and carnage of a human battle," Thoreau's attention is not that of an entomologist describing their behavior objectively, but rather that of a philosopher thinking about the universal urge to destroy.

The resemblance between animals and humans also works in the other direction, as when Thoreau describes the townsmen he sees on a trip to Concord as resembling prairie dogs. Ironically, the humans Thoreau describes often seem more "brutish" (like the authorities who imprison him in Concord) than the actual brutes in the woods do. Furthermore, Thoreau's intimacy with animals in *Walden* shows that solitude for him is not really, and not meant to be, total isolation. His very personal relationship with animals demonstrates that in his solitary stay at the pond, he is making more connections, not fewer, with other beings around him.

ICE

Since ice is the only product of Walden Pond that is useful, it becomes a symbol of the social use and social importance of nature, and of the exploitation of natural resources. Thoreau's fascination with the ice industry is acute. He describes in great detail the Irish icemen who arrive from Cambridge in the winter of 1846 to cut, block, and haul away 10,000 tons of ice for use in city homes and fancy hotels. The ice-cutters are the only group of people ever said to arrive at Walden Pond en masse, and so they inevitably represent society in miniature, with all the calculating exploitations and injustices that Thoreau sees in the world at large. Consequently, the labor of the icemen on Walden becomes a symbolic microcosm of the confrontation of society and nature. At first glance it would appear that society gets the upper hand, as the frozen pond is chopped up, disfigured, and robbed of ten thousand tons of its contents. But nature triumphs in the end, since less than twenty-five percent of the ice ever reaches its destination, the rest melting and evaporating en route— and making its way back to Walden Pond. With this analysis, Thoreau suggests that humankind's efforts to exploit nature are in vain, since nature regenerates itself on a far grander scale than humans could ever hope to affect, much less threaten. The icemen's exploitation of Walden contrasts sharply with Thoreau's less economic, more poetical use of it. In describing the rare mystical blue of Walden's water when frozen, he makes ice into a lyrical subject rather than a commodity, and makes us reflect on the question of the value, both market and spiritual, of nature in general.

Summary & Analysis

Economy

The mass of men lead lives of quiet desperation.

(See QUOTATIONS, p. 61)

Summary

Thoreau begins by matter-of-factly outlining his two-year project at Walden Pond, near Concord, Massachusetts (on land owned by his spiritual mentor Ralph Waldo Emerson, although Thoreau does not mention this detail). He says he lived there for two years and two months, and then moved back to "civilized society"—thus acknowledging right away, and quite honestly, that this was not a permanent lifestyle choice, but only an experiment in living. He describes the reactions of people to news of his project, noting their concern for his well-being out in the wilderness, their worry about his health in the winter, their shock that anyone would willingly forsake human companionship, and occasionally their envy. Thoreau moves quickly to the moral of his experiment: to illustrate the benefits of a simplified lifestyle. He tells us he is recounting the rudimentary existence he led there so that others might see the virtue of it. He argues that excess possessions not only require excess labor to purchase them, but also oppress us spiritually with worry and constraint. As people suppose they need to own things, this need forces them to devote all their time to labor, and the result is the loss of inner freedom. Thoreau asserts that, in their own way, farmers are chained to their farms just as much as prisoners are chained in jails. Working more than is necessary for subsistence shackles people. Faced with a choice between increasing one's means to acquire alleged necessities and decreasing one's needs, Thoreau believes minimizing one's needs is preferable by far. Thoreau identifies only four necessities: food, shelter, clothing, and fuel. Since nature itself does much to provide these, a person willing to accept the basic gifts of nature can live off the land with minimal toil. Any attempt at luxury is likely to prove more a hindrance than a help to an individual's improvement.

Thoreau describes the construction of his small house as an application of his faith in simplicity and self-reliance. Starting with nothing, Thoreau must even borrow the axe he needs to fell trees, an axe that he later returns (eager never to appear indebted to anyone) sharper than when he got it. He receives gifts of some supplies, purchasing others, and sets to work slowly but steadily through the spring months. Thoreau is ready to move in on July 4, 1845, the day of his own independence from social norms and conventions. Throughout the construction process and the agricultural endeavors that follow, Thoreau keeps meticulous books that he shares with us, accounting for all his debits and credits literally down to the last penny. He explains that in farming, after an investment of roughly fifteen dollars, he is able to turn a profit of almost nine dollars. He describes the diet of beans, corn, peas, and potatoes that sustains him, giving us the market value for all these foodstuffs as well. Overall, Thoreau's review of his own accounts reveals approximately sixty-two dollars of expenses during his first eight months at Walden, offset by a gain of almost thirty-seven dollars. Thus, at a total cost of just over twenty-five dollars, Thoreau acquires a home and the freedom to do as he pleases—a handsome bargain, in his opinion.

House,	$28 12 $\frac{1}{2}$
Farm one year,	14 72 $\frac{1}{2}$
Food eight months,	8 74
Clothing &c., eight months,	8 40 $\frac{3}{4}$
Oil, &c., eight months,	2 00
In all,	$61 99 $\frac{3}{4}$

(See QUOTATIONS, p. 62)

ANALYSIS

The first chapter of *Walden* offers an introduction to the oddball hodgepodge of styles, allusions, and subject matter that the work as a whole offers us. Thoreau moves from moral gravity to the style of a how-to manual, and then to a lyrical flight of fancy, and then to a diary entry. In a prophetic vein he tells us that his Walden experiment was intended to instruct his fellow men, who "labor under a mistake" about life, work, and leisure. But soon afterward, he tells us we may expect to spend $3.14 on nails if we build a shack of our own. And then, just as unexpectedly, he quotes the poet Chapman telling us how "for earthly greatness / All heavenly comforts rarefies to air." He can speak like a philosopher, using grand polysyllabic words, or he can talk quite simply about sitting on a pumpkin. It is never obvious whether this is the diary of a private experience, a sermon delivered to his compatriots, an extended fantasy about life in the woods, or a piece of nature writing. The common denominator of all this patchwork is the distinctive voice of Thoreau himself, who is the true subject of this work. Rather than a handbook for good living, *Walden* might best be read as a subjective extravaganza on the subject of Henry David Thoreau.

Reading the work as a personal fantasia rather than as a manual or sermon allows us to brush aside a lot of the criticism that has been aimed at *Walden* from its first publication until now. Some readers enjoy pointing out the failure of his project, how contradictory it is to claim self-reliance when he builds a shack on another man's property with borrowed tools and gifts of lumber, and how self-centered Thoreau seems throughout the work. Yet Thoreau himself never denies any of these accusations. He tells us in the first paragraph of "Economy" that his Walden project was only a temporary experiment, not a lifelong commitment to an ideal. He never claims to be a model socialist or a pioneer hero; he never even claims to be a very successful farmer or house-builder. Nor does he ever claim to eschew society altogether; on the contrary, he tells us that he never had more company than when he went to live in the woods, and that he goes to the village every day. As for self-reliance, he is content merely to have acquired a house for little money, relying more or less on his own labor, and is not an extremist about never seeking help from others (though he always aims to return favors). Self-reliance for Thoreau is more than paying one's own bills without debt; it is the spiritual pleasure of fully claiming ownership over the world in which one lives. Finally, Thoreau would happily admit the charge of self-centeredness: he exults in his vision and in the depths of his mind and soul. The vitality of this first chapter makes us ponder whether a lively sense of being centered in one's world is such a bad thing after all.

SUMMARY & ANALYSIS

WHERE I LIVED,
AND WHAT I LIVED FOR

*I went to the woods because I wished to live
deliberately, to front only the essential facts of life . . .
and not, when I came to die, discover that I had not
lived.* (See QUOTATIONS, p. 63)

SUMMARY

Thoreau recalls the several places where he nearly settled before
selecting Walden Pond, all of them estates on a rather large scale.
He quotes the Roman philosopher Cato's warning that it is best to
consider buying a farm very carefully before signing the papers. He
had been interested in the nearby Hollowell farm, despite the many
improvements that needed to be made there, but, before a deed
could be drawn, the owner's wife unexpectedly decided she wanted
to keep the farm. Consequently, Thoreau gave up his claim on the
property. Even though he had been prepared to farm a large tract,
Thoreau realizes that this outcome may have been for the best.
Forced to simplify his life, he concludes that it is best "as long as
possible" to "live free and uncommitted." Thoreau takes to the
woods, dreaming of an existence free of obligations and full of leisure. He proudly announces that he resides far from the post office
and all the constraining social relationships the mail system repre-
sents. Ironically, this renunciation of legal deeds provides him with
true ownership, paraphrasing a poet to the effect that "I am mon-
arch of all I survey."

Thoreau's delight in his new building project at Walden is more
than merely the pride of a first-time homeowner; it is a grandly
philosophic achievement in his mind, a symbol of his conquest of
being. When Thoreau first moves into his dwelling on Independence
Day, it gives him a proud sense of being a god on Olympus, even
though the house still lacks a chimney and plastering. He claims that
a paradise fit for gods is available everywhere, if one can perceive it:
"Olympus is but the outside of the earth every where." Taking an
optimistic view, he declares that his poorly insulated walls give his
interior the benefit of fresh air on summer nights. He justifies its lack
of carved ornament by declaring that it is better to carve "the very
atmosphere" one thinks and feels in, in an artistry of the soul. It is
for him an almost immaterial, heavenly house, "as far off as many a
region viewed nightly by astronomers." He prefers to reside here,

sitting on his own humble wooden chair, than in some distant corner
of the universe, "behind the constellation of Cassiopeia's Chair." He
is free from time as well as from matter, announcing grandiosely
that time is a river in which he goes fishing. He does not view himself
as the slave of time; rather he makes it seem as though he is choosing
to participate in the flow of time whenever and however he chooses,
like a god living in eternity. He concludes on a sermonizing note,
urging all of us to sludge through our existence until we hit rock bottom and can gauge truth on what he terms our "Realometer," our
means of measuring the reality of things

ANALYSIS
The title of this chapter combines a practical topic of residence
("Where I Lived") with what is probably the deepest philosophical
topic of all, the meaning of life ("What I Lived For"). Thoreau thus
reminds us again that he is neither practical do-it-yourself aficio-
nado nor erudite philosopher, but a mixture of both at once, attend-
ing to matters of everyday existence *and* to questions of final
meaning and purpose. This chapter pulls away from the bookkeeping lists and details about expenditures on nails and door hinges,
and opens up onto the more transcendent vista of how it all matters,
containing less how-to advice and much more philosophical meditation and grandiose universalizing assertion. It is here that we see
the full influence of Ralph Waldo Emerson on Thoreau's project.
Emersonian self-reliance is not just a matter of supporting oneself
financially (as many people believe) but a much loftier doctrine
about the active role that every soul plays in its experience of reality.
Reality for Emerson was not a set of objective facts in which we are
plunked down, but rather an emanation of our minds and souls that
create the world around ourselves every day.

Thoreau's building of a house on Walden Pond is, for him, a miniature re-enactment of God's creation of the world. He describes its
placement in the cosmos, in a region viewed by the astronomers, just
as God created a world within the void of space. He says outright
that he resides in his home as if on Mount Olympus, home of the
gods. He claims a divine freedom from the flow of time, describing
himself as fishing in its river. Thoreau's point in all this divine talk is
not to inflate his own personality to godlike heights but rather to
insist on everyone's divine ability to create a world. Our capacity to
choose reality is evident in his metaphor of the "Realometer," a

spin-off of the Nilometer, a device used to measure the depth of the river Nile. Thoreau urges us to wade through the muck that constitutes our everyday lives until we come to a firm place "which we can call Reality, and say, This is." The stamp of existence we give to our vision of reality—"This is"—evokes God's simple language in the creation story of Genesis: "Let there be. . . ." And the mere fact that Thoreau imagines that one can *choose* to call one thing reality and another thing not provides the spiritual freedom that was central to Emerson's Transcendentalist thought. When we create and claim this reality, all the other "news" of the world shrinks immediately to insignificance, as Thoreau illustrates in his mocking parody of newspapers reporting a cow run over by the Western Railway. He opines that the last important bit of news to come out of England was about the revolution of 1649, almost two centuries earlier. The only current events that matter to the transcendent mind are itself and its place in the cosmos.

SUMMARY

One of the many delightful pursuits in which Thoreau is able to indulge, having renounced a big job and a big mortgage, is reading. He has grand claims for the benefits of reading, which he compares, following ancient Egyptian or Hindu philosophers, to "raising the veil from the statue of divinity." Whether or not Thoreau is ironic in such monumental reflections about books is open to debate, but it is certain that reading is one of his chief pastimes in the solitude of the woods, especially after the main construction work is done. During the busy days of homebuilding, he says he kept Homer's *Iliad* on his table throughout the summer, but only glanced at it now and then. But now that he has moved in not just to his handmade shack, but into the full ownership of reality described in the preceding chapter, reading has a new importance. Thoreau praises the ability to read the ancient classics in the original Greek and Latin, disdaining the translations offered by the "modern cheap" press. Indeed he goes so far as to assert that Homer has never yet been published in English— at least not in any way that does justice to Homer's achievement. Thoreau emphasizes the work of reading, just as he stresses the work of farming and home-owning; he compares the great reader to an athlete who has subjected himself to long training and regular exercise. He gives an almost mystical importance to the printed word. The grandeur of oratory does not impress him as much as the achievements of a written book. He says it is no wonder that Alexander the Great carried a copy of the *Iliad* around with him on his military campaigns.

Thoreau also urges us to read widely, gently mocking those who limit their reading to the Bible, and to read great things, not the popular entertainment books found in the library. Thoreau gradually extends his criticism of cheap reading to a criticism of the dominant culture of Concord, which deprives even the local gifted minds access to great thought. Despite the much-lauded progress of modern society in technology and transportation, he says real progress—that of the mind and soul—is being forgotten. He reproaches his townsmen for believing that the ancient Hebrews were the only people in the world to have had a Holy Scripture, ignoring the sacred writings of others, like the Hindus. Thoreau complains the townspeople spend more on any body ailment than they do on mental malnourishment; he calls out, like an angry prophet, for more public spending on education. He says, "New England can hire all the wise men in the world to come and teach her, and board them round the while, and not be provincial at all." Thoreau implicitly blames the local class system for encouraging fine breeding in noblemen but neglecting the task of ennobling the broader population. He thus calls out for an aristocratic democracy: "[i]nstead of noblemen, let us have noble villages of men."

ANALYSIS

This chapter shows us how subtly Thoreau can segue from the personal to the public, and from observation to diatribe. He begins by simply stating that now that the work on his house has been finished, he has time to read the Homeric epic that has been sitting on his table untouched all summer. Reading here seems broached as a private pastime, an entertainment for the individual mind after the day's work is done. But little by little he moves from the particular to the general, commenting not just on his ability to read Homer in the original but on the merits of *all* people being able to do so. This point leads him to a meditation on modern publishing and its stultification of the American audience, which in turn leads him to a bitter reflection on the parochialism of his compatriots who do not even know that the Hindus have a sacred writing like that of the Hebrews. By the end of the chapter, he has driven himself into a thunderous rage—as the large number of rhetorically powerful question marks and exclamation marks in the last paragraph suggest—over the American prejudice against education. He begins in the individual mode, referring to *his* copy of the *Iliad* and *his* leisure time. But by the end the reference has shifted to "we" rather than "I," so that the word "us" is the last word of the chapter, appearing in the gloomy and despairing image of "the gulf of ignorance that surrounds us." Thoreau begins the chapter as a quiet meditation about an evening's reading pleasure but somehow ends it as a raging sermon about the state of the world.

It is in this chapter that Thoreau's social background is most fully felt, especially the advantages of a Harvard education and a familiarity with the classics and with ancient languages. Earlier in the work, his words do not betray his origins; in discussing home construction or domestic economy, he is simply a fiery thinker and a practical man. But when he discourses on the necessity of reading Aeschylus in the original Greek, disdaining the contemporary translations offered by the "modern cheap and fertile press," we feel that he is a member of the elite speaking to us. Although he calls out at the end of the chapter for "noble villages of men" in which education is spread broadly through the population instead of thinly over the aristocrats, we feel he must realize the impracticality of expecting woodcutters to read Aeschylus in Greek. This tension introduces the dark subject of Thoreau's snobbism, which recurs later in his exchange with John Field and his family. Thoreau may sincerely appreciate the merits of poverty and values the lifestyle of common laborers, but his lofty words about the classics recall that in fact he is a Harvard-educated man slumming in the backwoods, and that his poverty is chosen rather than forced on him by circumstances.

SOUNDS AND SOLITUDE

SUMMARY: SOUNDS

As if dispelling the bookish air of the preceding chapter, Thoreau begins to praise a sharp alertness to existence and cautions against absorption in old epic poems. "Will you be a reader, a student merely, or a seer?" he asks, making it clear that we should not be content with book-learning, but should look around and "see" things in our lives. But these things we are to "see" are not grand ideas; the sort of vision Thoreau has in mind is that of idle sitting on a doorstep in the warm sunlight, as he describes himself doing. He hears a sparrow chirp, and contemplates the sumac and some other plants.

Thoreau's tranquility is interrupted by the "scream" of the Fitchburg Railroad, which passes near his home. His thoughts turn to commerce. While he lauds the active resourcefulness, even calling it "bravery," of tradesmen, he fears that an excessive zeal for business will ruin the wit and thoughtfulness of the nation. On Sundays Thoreau hears the bells of churches. At night he often hears the owls, "midnight hags," whose moans he interprets as *Oh-o-o-o that I never had been bor-r-r-n!* He rejoices that owls exist, for they can do their "idiotic and maniacal hooting" for men, voicing the "unsatisfied thoughts which all have." Thoreau notes that even without a rooster or any other kept animals, his home is full of the sounds of beasts. Nature is creeping up, he says, to his very windowsill.

SUMMARY: SOLITUDE
Thoreau describes a "delicious evening" in which he feels at one with nature, "a part of herself." It is cool and windy, but nevertheless the bullfrogs and night animals give it a special charm. When he returns to his home, he finds that visitors have passed by and left small gifts and tokens. Thoreau remarks that even though his closest neighbor is only a mile away, he may as well be in Asia or Africa, so great is his feeling of solitude. Paradoxically, he is not alone in his solitude, since he is "suddenly sensible of such sweet and beneficent society in Nature . . . as made the fancied advantages of human neighborhood insignificant." It is not that he is giving up society, but rather that he is exchanging the "insignificant" society of humans for the superior society of nature. He explains that loneliness can occur even amid companions if one's heart is not open to them. Thoreau meditates on the deep pleasure he feels in escaping the gossips of the town. Instead of their poisonous company, he has the company of an old settler who lives nearby and tells him mystical stories of "old time and new eternity," and the company of an old woman whose "memory runs back farther than mythology." It is unclear whether these companions are real or imaginary. Thoreau again praises the benefits of nature and of his deep communion with it. He maintains that the only medicine he needs in life is a draught of morning air.

ANALYSIS
While the preceding chapter on reading emphasizes the connections between the individual and society (if not the inferior society of

Concord, then the grand society of great past authors), these two chapters focus on the individual by himself. Yet, paradoxically, this removal from society does not mean that Thoreau is alone, for he continually asserts that nature offers better society than humans do. What Thoreau means by "solitude," we discover, is not loneliness or isolation, but rather self-communion and introspection. It has little to do with the physical proximity of others, since he says that a man can be lonely when surrounded by others if he does not feel real companionship with them.

Solitude is thus more a state of mind than an actual physical circumstance, and for Thoreau it approaches a mystical state. Solitude means that he is on his own spiritually, confronting the full array of nature's bounty without any intermediaries. The importance of worldly affairs, even the ones that occupy him in the first chapters, fades. Far less activity, whether physical or mental, occupies these chapters, than had occupied earlier ones. Thoreau is emptying his life of busy work in order to confront the reality of the cosmos. There are no more messages from great minds to decipher; Thoreau here does not listen to another's words or heed another's authority, but rather perceives empty sounds like the hooting of owls, the scream of the Fitchburg train, and the bells of the local church. These sounds are different from the words of Aeschylus and Homer mentioned in the last chapter not only because they are audible rather than silent, but also because they have no wisdom or message to convey. The wail of the train does not signify anything; it merely wails. The sparrow chirps, but there is no clue as to what, if anything, it wishes to communicate.

Unlike the earlier vision of an existence full of ideas and meanings, these chapters offer a vision of a universe strangely absurd, a "tale told by an idiot," to echo *Macbeth*, as Thoreau is consciously doing. Thoreau describes the owls' hooting as "idiotic and maniacal," and he compares the nocturnal birds to "midnight hags," referring directly to Macbeth's description of the three witches as "secret black and midnight hags" (IV, i, 63). And just as the witches express Macbeth's deep unconscious desire for kingship, so too is Thoreau grateful to the owls for voicing the "unsatisfied thoughts" that men cannot express consciously. Macbeth's vision of a chaotic and violent universe may seem to have little to do with Thoreau's tranquil mood in these chapters. But his emphatic allusions to Shakespeare's play suggest that the basic idea of the mysterious and inscrutable universe is the same in both, as well as the idea that the individual human mind is the source of meaning in it, for good or for bad. Thus Thoreau praises the idea of being a "seer," just as Macbeth is a visionary hero who sees himself king of Scotland and sees an imaginary dagger before his eyes. Macbeth creates a mental vision of horror that becomes reality for him; Thoreau is also creating a vision of himself similarly powerful and independent, but without succumbing to the voices of the hags.

VISITORS

SUMMARY

Thoreau states that he likes companionship as much as anyone else, and keeps three chairs ready for visitors. But he is aware of the limitations of his small house, aware that "individuals, like nations, must have suitable broad and natural boundaries." Thus he often moves the conversation to the pine forest outside his door. As a host he is not conventional. He is not concerned with offering savory delicacies to his guests, and if there is not enough food to go around, he and his guests go without. Caring more about providing his visitors spiritual, rather than material, sustenance, Thoreau proudly comments that he could nourish a thousand as easily as twenty. If they go away hungry afterward, he says, at least they have his sympathy.

Yet despite such discomforts, Thoreau's guests keep coming. Indeed he says he has more visitors than he used to have when living in town. And the overall quality of his socializing has improved as well. Because of his relative isolation, those visitors whom Thoreau does receive are rarely on trivial errands, so that the less interesting ones are "winnowed," as he puts it, from the better ones. They make the considerable journey from town only if they are deeply committed to seeing him. He also meets an interesting collection of vagabonds and wayfarers. Thoreau often finds admirable qualities in these rude characters, and sees them as agreeable, deferential visitors. In contrast, Thoreau disdains beggars, remarking that "objects of charity are not guests." He entertains children on berry-picking expeditions. As an ardent abolitionist, he is also inclined to help runaway slaves on the Underground Railway, though he does not boast about it.

Thoreau also receives visits from those living or working nearby. Among them he gives special attention to a French Canadian-born woodsman of happy and unpretentious ways, identified by scholars as a certain Alex Therien. Unlike Thoreau, Therien cannot read or write. Thoreau describes him as living an "animal life," and admires his physical endurance and his ability to amuse himself. Thoreau notes that Therien was never educated to the level of "consciousness," but that on occasion he reveals a wisdom all his own. Reluctant to expound his ideas and unable to write them down, Therien is humble and modest. Still, Therien reveals at times "a certain positive originality, however slight," suggesting to Thoreau that perhaps "there might be men of genius in the lowest grades of life." He compares Therien to Walden Pond itself, saying that Therien's mind is as deep as Walden is "bottomless," though it may appear "dark and muddy."

Thoreau notes that women and children appear to enjoy the woods more than men. He says men of business, and even farmers, tend to focus not on the pleasures of rural life, but on its limitations, such as the distance from town. Even when they claim to like walks in the forest, Thoreau can see that they do not. Their lives are all taken up, he says, with "getting a living," and they do not have the time to live.

ANALYSIS

The visitors mentioned in this chapter's title do not interfere with the preceding "Solitude," because Thoreau's ideal guests do not interrupt one's self-communion but merely broaden it. Concerned that socializing not limit one's personal space or elbowroom, he describes how his guests push their chairs as far away from each as possible, as far as the walls of his house allow. When this area is not sufficient, they take the chat outdoors. Thoreau refers to a conversation as if it were a physical thing, like a football game, requiring a large playing field; he describes "the difficulty of getting to a sufficient distance from my guest" when conversation turns philosophical. But, of course, Thoreau is speaking metaphorically here, and the space required for a good talk is mental rather than physical. More than a practical issue of space management, it is a philosophical statement about every human's need for freedom to stretch his or her soul. It is even a political statement as well, since Thoreau says that nations are the same way, perhaps alluding to the American pioneers' westward expansion. When he recommends an outdoor conversation in the pine trees, Thoreau argues that a good conversation could expand to fill the whole forest or perhaps the whole universe.

Thoreau's characterization of his various guests shows us a lot about his social and moral views as well. We find out his opposition to slavery when he mentions, almost in passing, that he occasionally aids fugitive slaves. That he does not boast about this shows his humility. We see that Thoreau has a well-developed sense of hospitality toward strangers, irrespective of class or occupation; he welcomes wayfarers of all sorts. He is no snob in his admission of visitors, at a time when the game of calling cards and the ranking of guests was a standard part of civilized life. But his treatment of beggars is a bit surprising. When he declares that "objects of charity are not our guests," he obviously means that no equality is possible between a beggar and a homeowner, but he also seems uncomfortably close to saying that the desperately poor do not deserve the same respect as better-off travelers. Thoreau does have some prejudices. His attitude toward the Canadian-born woodcutter Alex Therien also reveals a somewhat unjust discrimination against the uneducated, even as he appears to appreciate the man. At first Thoreau praises Therien as a Homeric figure, larger than life, possessing noble instincts and a generous heart. He appreciates that Therien loves his work and displays good humor at every turn. He even says that Therien displays a kind of unformed natural genius. But then Thoreau suddenly demotes Therien from epic hero to animal. Of course, Thoreau loves animals, and his remark is not meant as an insult. But his assessment that Therien is "too immersed in his animal life" indicates that Thoreau is unable or unwilling to treat him as an equal. We imagine Thoreau saying to himself that, being educated, he deserves to have poets and philosophers as his guests, and the bestiality of Therien—no matter how much of a genius he is in his animal state—somehow makes him an inappropriate companion. Thoreau may go off to live in nature, but he cannot bring himself to call a natural man his equal.

THE BEAN-FIELD

SUMMARY

Thoreau plants two and a half acres of beans, along with smaller amounts of potatoes, turnips, and peas, and farms them throughout the summer months. Working barefoot, he lays out his plot, pausing at times to observe the wildlife around him. He hoes his beans each day and settles into the daily routine of the farm worker. The rains that come help his crops, but the woodchucks destroy a significant portion of them. Thoreau, anticipating that the soil of his bean plot will be rich, discovers that "an extinct nation had anciently dwelt here and planted corn and beans ere white men came to clear the land, and so, to some extent, had exhausted the soil for this very crop." Thoreau finds evidence of this previous occupation everywhere, excavating arrowheads, shards of pottery, and other artifacts among the "ashes of unchronicled nations" while digging.

Thoreau often leans on his hoe and enjoys the "inexhaustible entertainment" of his environment, the sights and sounds of nature. But he also hears military exercises echoing from the nearby town, resounding across the bean-field. Thoreau says he finds himself reassured on such days, confident that his liberties would be defended in the event of a conflict. Thoreau says that, on hearing the gunfire, "I felt as if I could spit a Mexican with a good relish ... and looked around for a woodchuck or a skunk to exercise my chivalry upon." In his rural enclave, however, he feels distant from the necessity of war.

In all, Thoreau spends just under fifteen dollars on his crops, earning almost twenty-four dollars and making a profit of almost nine dollars. No great eater of beans himself, he barters most of his crop for rice, keeping the turnips and peas for his own sustenance. In providing advice on husbandry, Thoreau recommends fresh soil, vigilance against pests, and an early harvest that beats the first frost. But despite the profit he makes, Thoreau states that his purpose in cultivating crops is not so much to earn money but to develop self-discipline. He says that it is the cultivation of the farmer, and not the crop, that makes husbandry a worthwhile pursuit. Thoreau marvels that people care so intently about the success of their farms and so little about the state of the "crop" of men.

Thoreau reflects that nature does not care whether the year's crop succeeds or fails, as the sun shines on plowed and fallow ground alike. Thoreau maintains that part of any crop is meant as a sacrifice to the woodchuck. Although the field infested with weeds is a curse to the hungry farmer, Thoreau says it is a blessing to the hungry bird. In such a world, Thoreau concludes, the farmer should not feel anxious, but should simply accept the blessings that nature bestows upon him.

ANALYSIS

The mythical side of Thoreau's Walden venture is clearly evident in the imagery he borrows from classical mythology to describe his bean cultivation. Downplaying or even ignoring the pragmatic aspect of farming or its actual results (the harvest), Thoreau makes agriculture into a symbolic and transcendent activity. It has a "constant and imperishable moral," as if it were an exercise in morality rather than a pursuit of material sustenance. He remarks that manual labor "to the scholar yields a classic result," dubbing himself an industrious farmer, or *agricola laboriosus*, in Latin. We feel that Thoreau is more interested in the classical role he is playing than in the actual beans he will one day reap. Similarly, when Thoreau refers to his hard work in hoeing the fields, he compares himself to the Greek mythological figure of a North African giant who wrestled with Hercules. He remarks that "[m]y beans ... attached me to the earth, and so I got strength like Antaeus," emphasizing the sheer vitality rather than the material productivity of his endeavors.

Thoreau compares farming to art as well, repeatedly referring to the music produced by his hoe as it strikes the earth rather than to the agricultural benefits of hoeing. He states that "my hoe played the *Ranz des Vaches*," a French folk song, with the beans as his audience. Similarly, he describes himself as "dabbling like a plastic artist in the dewy and crumbling sand." The point of all these references to myth and art is that they emphasize the impracticality of Thoreau's agricultural efforts and by extension his whole stay at Walden Pond.

The religious symbolism of his farming is equally apparent. Unlike the typical subsistence farmer, who would clearly understand the end result of his work, Thoreau claims not even to know the point or final goal of all his labor. He asks, "Why should I raise them? Only Heaven knows." In acknowledging that God alone knows why he is engaged in bean cultivation, Thoreau is ignoring the material side of farming and transforming it into an almost biblical parable about the mysteries of human endeavor on earth: we cannot claim to know why we live, for only God knows. Like the Book of Ecclesiastes, which says that for every human life there is a time to reap and a time to sow, the emphasis here is on the mystical and symbolic process of agriculture rather than on the market value of its saleable products. Thus the careful calculations found in the first chapter, "Economy," and later in this chapter (reporting that a hoe costs fifty-four cents), seem less important when he says he does not even know why he is farming: calculations do not matter when the end result is not important. In fact he claims that in the future he will not sow beans at all but will rather practice an agriculture of morals, sowing "such seeds ... as sincerity, truth, simplicity, faith, innocence, and the like." In short, although Thoreau's mythical bean-field allusions majestically enhance the spiritual and philosophical side of his Walden project and of the work we are reading, it also undermines Thoreau's frequent attempts to portray his ideas as the simple and practical-minded thoughts of any common field worker close to nature. Inspirational and thought-provoking as his literary work is, it is certainly not the product of the mind of an ordinary New England small farmer.

Thoreau's discovery that his bean-fields are on the site of ancient Native American plots gives an interesting, multicultural touch to this chapter, which is full of Greek, Roman, and biblical allusions from Western culture. But he does not claim that the land belongs to the original inhabitants any more than it belongs to the invading westerners. The soil he cultivates is full of Native American artifacts, but they mingle with "bits of pottery and glass brought hither by the recent cultivators." The land, in other words, is a mixed bag of traces of different cultures, a mosaic of different origins. He thus shows little interest in claiming it belongs purely and singly to any culture, native or European. This apathy implies a non-possessive attitude. Unlike many American settlers who claimed an absolute right to their conquered homesteads, Thoreau views himself as an interloper in territories that are not his own: "I disturbed the ashes of unchronicled nations who in primeval years lived under these heavens." He is not quite apologizing for intruding upon alien lands, but is at least registering that he is disturbing the spirits (or at least the remains) of others who came before him. Since many early Americans believed that white people brought culture to a virgin land, Thoreau shows a forward-thinking fairness in acknowledging that he is only one in a long line of people who have lived on this land since "primeval years." His focus is on living in harmony with the land rather than on asserting some idea of cultural ownership over it.

THE VILLAGE AND THE PONDS

SUMMARY: THE VILLAGE

Around noon, after his morning chores are finished, Thoreau takes a second bath in the pond and prepares to spend the rest of his day at leisure. Several times a week he hikes into Concord, where he gathers the latest gossip and meets with townsmen at the main centers of activity, the grocery, the bar, the post office, and the bank. Stores of all kinds try to seduce him with their advertised wares, but Thoreau has no interest in consumer splurges, and makes his way back home without lingering too long in the marketplace. He often makes his way back to Walden Pond in the dark, which is challenging. But with practice he grows accustomed to the way, feeling his path out by the neighboring trees or the rut of the path below. Other people, he notes, are not as adapted to nighttime walking. Even in the village itself, he says, many lose their way in the darkness, sometimes wandering for hours. Thoreau does not consider such dislocation to be a bad thing. Through being lost, he says, one truly comes to understand oneself and "the infinite extent of our relations."

On one of his journeys into Concord, Thoreau is detained, arrested, and jailed for his refusal to pay a poll tax to "the state which buys and sells men, women, and children, like cattle at the door of its senate-house." After a night in jail he is released, and returns to Walden Pond, remarkably unexcited about his incarceration. Thoreau calmly muses about how, except for governmental intrusion, he lives without fear of being disturbed by anyone. He does not find it necessary to lock up his own possessions and always welcomes visitors of all classes. He says that theft exists only in communities where "some have got more than is sufficient while others have not enough."

SUMMARY: THE PONDS

*A field of water betrays the spirit that is in the air. It is
continually receiving new life and motion from above.
It is intermediate between land and sky.*
(See QUOTATIONS, p. 64)

When Thoreau has enough of town life, he spends his leisure time in the country. At times Thoreau takes a boat on the pond and plays his flute, and he goes fishing at midnight as well, drifting between waking and dreaming until he snaps awake when he feels a tug on his line. This fishing vignette allows Thoreau to segue into an extended meditation on the local Concord ponds, especially Walden.

Although Walden Pond itself is not particularly grand, Thoreau says, it is remarkably deep and pure. Depending on the point of view and the time of day, the water of the pond may appear blue, green, or totally transparent. It makes the body of the bather appear pure white, rather than yellowish as the river water does. Thoreau reports that Walden Pond is said by some to be bottomless. White stones surround the shore, allowing Thoreau to venture a wry etymology of its name ("walled-in"), and hills rise beyond. Other ponds, such as Flints', have their distinctive qualities, and Thoreau's emphasis is on their uniqueness rather than their generic similarities.

In exploring the outlying areas, Thoreau notes the well-worn paths of previous generations now long gone. He comments on the unpredictable fluctuations in the depth of the pond, and speculates on some possible origins of the name Walden. Thoreau muses about how his fellow townsmen think the pond resulted from the sinking of a hill into the earth as punishment for Native American wrongdoing that took place there. He says that his "ancient settler" friend, referred to earlier in the work, claims to have dug the pond. Thoreau says that he does not object to these stories. He notices that the surrounding hills contain the same kind of stones that surround Walden's walled-in shores. Animals found at the pond, including ducks, frogs, muskrats, minks, and turtles, all make an appearance in Thoreau's account. Growing more mystical by the end of the chapter, Thoreau focuses on the serenity and peacefulness of the ponds in a way that suggests a higher meaning. He says that they are beyond human description or knowledge, and are "much more beautiful than our lives."

ANALYSIS: THE VILLAGE AND THE PONDS

On Walden Pond Thoreau is no misanthrope, but indulges quite freely in his taste for social interaction, as his interactions with the village indicate. He heads off to the village every day not for the practical purpose of gathering supplies, but simply "to hear some of the gossip which is incessantly going on there," which he finds "as refreshing in its way as the rustle of leaves and the peeping of frogs." This statement is revealing, showing that Thoreau neither dismisses nor overvalues human society, neither rejecting it totally nor finding anything more important than gossip in it. Instead, he places it on the same level as frogs and leaves, without much meaning but pleasant in its own limited way. When compared to nature, society seems nice and harmless. Thoreau makes himself a kind of naturalist of social life, perceiving humans as creatures in their native habitat. Men on the main street appear to him "as curious to me as if they had been prairie-dogs, each sitting at the mouth of its burrow." His remark that ordinary villagers strike him as "curious" echoes similar remarks that the townspeople make elsewhere about Thoreau himself: that he is a freak for wanting to live so far from town. Thoreau is showing that social existence also has its own peculiar strangeness and that being isolated on Walden Pond is no more bizarre than living like a prairie dog in town.

Yet social life for Thoreau is not always so peaceful and harmless. If the visitor loses his natural good sense within the village, and is seduced by its illusory appeals, it becomes a risky place to be. As Thoreau's description of the village's layout proceeds, it uses more and more words of aggression, onslaught, and danger. Every traveler has to "run the gauntlet," he says, when exploring the place. The houses are arranged as if in a battle-line, so that the villagers "might get a lick at" the visitor before he can "escape." Advertising signs "catch him." In portraying the dangers of village life, Thoreau is indirectly mocking the villagers' beliefs that it is nature that is hostile and threatening. Thoreau says that he has never been "distressed in any weather" out in the open, unlike the distraught townspeople who lose their way at night and stray far from the well-trod streets of the village. For Thoreau, being lost in this way is neither dangerous nor inadvisable. Being disoriented with regard to society—losing the path to the village—is far less serious, implies Thoreau, than being disoriented with regard to our own selves. It is better to find oneself and risk one's social standing, if need be, just as Thoreau himself does when as a conscientious objector he is jailed for nonpayment of a tax. In commenting on this point, he ironically reverses the idea that he is a wild rebel, saying instead that it is society that has "run amok" of him. His casual tone in reporting the jail incident ("One afternoon . . ." he begins coolly, as if relating another squirrel sighting or fishing trip) illustrates how unimportant it is in his life, which has generally been successful in "escap[ing]" not just jail but all social constraints.

Thoreau's description of Walden Pond in the beautiful "Ponds" chapter hints at a symbolic significance to this mysterious, deep, and pure body of water. Blue or green when seen from different angles, yet "as colorless as an equal quantity of air" when a glass of it is held up to the light, Walden Pond is profoundly indefinable. Thoreau mentions that some people "think it is bottomless," or infinitely deep. Other waters make the human bather appear yellowish, but Walden gives the human body an alabaster whiteness, like a figure by Michelangelo. Since Michelangelo was a religious artist, and white a Christian symbol of purity, Walden's infinity and mystery makes it seem divine. Indeed, water, in Christianity, through the sacrament of baptism, is a powerful symbol of a higher life in Christ. Thoreau is never an explicitly Christian writer, but subtly Walden Pond seems to perform some of the functions traditionally performed by the church. Its fascinating "glassy surface" reflects heaven, "a perfect forest mirror" of the sky above. It seems a little bit of heaven on earth, and the chapter's last line suggests that it is better than heaven, because it can be found on earth: "Talk of heaven! ye disgrace earth." The living human has access to and may choose to live near the earthly pond, as Thoreau does. In a sense the pond may represent the natural soul of humankind, a bit of heaven we can discover within us, "walled-in" within our external social selves, just as Walden is walled in by its stones.

BAKER FARM AND HIGHER LAWS

SUMMARY: BAKER FARM
Thoreau sometimes roams beyond Walden Pond and Flints' Pond to outlying groves and woods, surveying the land. One day, caught in a rainstorm on a fishing trip, Thoreau takes cover in a hut near Baker Farm that he imagines to be deserted. But inside he finds John Field and his family, poor Irish immigrants. A conversation ensues, although it is more a lecture by Thoreau to Field on how he should live his life, telling Field that if he reevaluates his priorities and economizes, he can pull himself out of poverty. Thoreau says that the wild state of nature is best and that "the only true America" is that place where one can do without luxuries such as tea, coffee, butter, and beef. Thoreau insists that he speaks to Field as a fellow philosopher, but Field is not overly receptive to Thoreau's points. Thoreau concludes that the Irishman is not interested in taking risks, and lacks the "arithmetic" to see the wisdom of Thoreau's financial management advice. He leaves the Field home with

no mention of having shared a moment of warmth or humor with the family. Moreover, Thoreau makes the unfair speculation that Field suffers from "inherited Irish poverty." Before departing, Thoreau notes that even the well is dirty, its rope broken, and its bucket "irrecoverable." Yet, having asked for a drink of water, Thoreau says he does not refuse the dirty "gruel" that "sustains life here." Thoreau proclaims, "I am not squeamish in such cases when manners are concerned."

Summary: Higher Laws

On the walk home, Thoreau passes a woodchuck, and is seized with a primitive desire to devour it. He notices his own dual nature, part noble and spiritual, part dark and savage, and declares that he values both sides of himself. Thoreau believes in the importance of the hunt as an early stage in a person's education and upbringing, noting that intellectual and spiritual individuals then move on to higher callings, leaving "the gun and fish-pole behind."

Although he is a skilled fisherman, Thoreau confesses his reluctance for the practice in recent days, borne of a sense that the fish is neither fully nourishing nor fully clean. His impulse toward vegetarianism, however, is based on his instincts and his principles rather than on any actual experience of poor health. Thoreau also avoids the consumption of alcohol, tea, and coffee on the same grounds. To him the simplest fare is the best, and the consumption of animal flesh is a moral debasement that far fewer would indulge in if they had to slaughter beasts themselves. Thoreau feels strongly that the minister should not partake of the hunt, and he himself finds grains and vegetables both more filling and less difficult to prepare. Thoreau says that one should delight in one's appetite, rather than obey it dutifully. Yet, while there is much to be gained from savoring a meal, taste should not be taken to the point of indulgence. Thus there is water to quench thirst, rather than wine. This simplicity of taste marks his other pleasures as well: Thoreau prefers a breath of fresh air to the strains of a musical composition.

Thoreau aspires to distinguish his higher nature from his more animalistic tendencies. It is never a fully successful effort, yet even in failure he says it is a pursuit that yields considerable rewards. As the animal nature fades, one approaches divinity. Thoreau says we have a choice: we may strive to be either chaste or sensual, either pure or impure. In the end, Thoreau says, it is up to each individual to care for his or her body and his or her soul, saying that "[e]very man is the builder of a temple." The proof of that care will be evident in the face and in the features, he says, which will acquire the visage of nobility when one engages in right thought and action and the visage of degradation when one engages in wrong thought and action. To conclude, Thoreau invokes the figure of John Farmer, an allegorical representation of the common man who hears the music of higher spheres, questions his life of hopeless toil, and decides to live his life with a "new austerity." Farmer "redeem[s]" himself by letting his "mind descend into his body," and becomes able to "treat himself with ever increasing respect."

ANALYSIS: BAKER FARM AND HIGHER LAWS

Most of the material in these two sections, and afterward, was added after Thoreau left Walden. In general, these sections were not begun in earnest until 1851, and Thoreau did not impose chapter divisions until 1853, more than five years after he abandoned his cabin in the woods. As a result, much of the writing that appears in the latter portion of *Walden* does not feel as closely related to his self-reliance project as the earlier chapters do, though they still remain connected by themes and ideas.

The Baker Farm episode raises questions that are central to the earlier part of the work, giving us the opportunity to see what happens when Thoreau applies his ideas about domestic economy onto the lives of others. Thoreau demonstrates a strange lack of generosity on his part when considering John Field and his family. He describes Mrs. Field's "round greasy face and bare breast," representing her as an ineffectual housekeeper "with the never absent mop in one hand, and yet no effects of it visible anywhere." Here, in a single breath, he is calling a woman who offers him shelter unwashed, unkempt, and unproductive—and with no apparent remorse. In a similarly ungenerous manner, he describes the Field baby as "wrinkled" and "cone-headed." And when this baby naturally regards Thoreau with the self-confidence of infancy, Thoreau sees not its sweet innocence, but rather its self-delusion in behaving as though it were "the last of a noble line, and the hope and cynosure of the world" instead of an ugly and malnourished creature. John Field himself is described as honest and hard working, but "shiftless," a poor money manager. This verdict, which is quite damning given Thoreau's insistence on keeping one's accounts simple and healthy, may explain the mild animosity he shows the family (perhaps without realizing it): the Fields are the negative examples of economy, while he is the positive example of it. That he himself once contemplated living on Baker Farm, as he tells us, and that he too is living in the backwoods on a subsistence level suggests that he sees the Fields as his counterparts. But the difference between him and the Fields is what matters most to Thoreau: they do not share his enlightened philosophy of self-reliance, and so they fail where he has succeeded.

Thoreau seems remarkably unfriendly in what he tells us of his interaction with this poor family. He does not chat with the Fields, but launches immediately into a lecture about how Thoreau's shanty cost as much to buy outright as the Fields spend annually on rent, and about how cutting down on coffee and meat would save them money. We can imagine the annoyance of such a guest appearing unannounced in one's home, handing out advice unsolicited. Furthermore, he leaves with no mention of sharing any human connection or having a laugh with the Fields. He merely asks for a drink of water (which he has to shut his eyes to gulp down, aware of its poor quality), and departs. This display of rudeness—not just in outward manners, but also in his categorical imposition of his own views on others without reporting their side of the story—forces us to see a side of Thoreau different from that of the solitary dreamer and conscientious objector we have seen before. Here we see that Thoreau's fervent convictions may actually stand in the way of human relations. Perhaps his isolation is making him not just self-reliant but also somewhat antisocial, or at least grossly insensitive to the situations of others. By idealizing and simplifying humans, as his allegorical depiction of "John Farmer" at the end of the chapter suggests, he may have difficulties thinking about the complexities of real people's lives.

One of the most distressing aspects of Thoreau's attitude toward the Fields is his focus on their Irish heritage, which he associates—in stereotypical nineteenth-century Anglo-American style—with laziness and self-neglect. In a final note of pity, he suggests that Field is poor not because he lacks Thoreau's advantages of education or because the plight of immigrants is difficult, but simply because he was "born to be poor." Thoreau almost implies a kind of racist belief in genetic predisposition to economic performance when he refers to Field's "inherited Irish poverty." The notion of free self-determination that Thoreau extols throughout *Walden* seems inapplicable, in his mind, to the poor Irish: with their inherited poverty, they can never break free to become self-reliant like he has. Thoreau praises poverty, but only when it is self-imposed rather than when it is determined by social forces. Combined with his curt treatment of the Fields, this prejudice leaves a bitter aftertaste. There is no brotherhood of the poor in his mind; Thoreau focuses on what separates himself and the Fields, and their Irish background is one difference. Thoreau's views on the causes of Irish poverty are startlingly conservative, given his much-vaunted status as a radical.

BRUTE NEIGHBORS AND HOUSE-WARMING

SUMMARY: BRUTE NEIGHBORS

Thoreau's good friend William Ellery Channing sometimes accompanied him on his fishing trips when Channing came out to Walden Pond from Concord. Thoreau creates a simplified version of one of their conversations, featuring a hermit (himself) and a poet (Channing). The poet is absorbed in the clouds in the sky, while the hermit is occupied with the more practical task of getting fish for dinner; at the end the poet regrets his failure to catch fish.

Thoreau plays with the mice that share his house, describing one that takes a bit of cheese from Thoreau's fingers. He also has regular encounters with a phoebe, a robin, and a partridge and her brood; he calls these wild birds his hens and chickens. Less frequently he sees otters and raccoons. Thoreau is struck by the raccoons' ability to live hidden in the woods while nevertheless sustaining themselves on the refuse of human neighborhoods. About a half-mile from his habitation, Thoreau digs a makeshift well to which he often goes after his morning's work to eat his lunch, gather fresh water, and read for a while. There he frequently encounters woodcocks and turtledoves.

On one occasion, Thoreau happens to notice a large black ant battling with a smaller red ant. Examining the scene more closely, he sees that it is actually part of a large conflict pitting an army of black ants against an army of red ants twice its number, but whose soldiers are half the size of the black army. Thoreau meditates on its resemblance to human wars, and concludes that the ants are just as fierce and spirited as human soldiers. Thoreau removes a wood chip, along with three ant combatants, from the scene of the battle, carrying it back to his cabin to observe it. He places them under a turned-over glass and brings a microscope to watch their struggle. After witnessing a pair of decapitations and some cannibalism, he releases the survivor.

Thoreau frequently encounters cats in the woods. Although domesticated, they prove quite comfortable in the woods, so inherently wild as to spit at Thoreau when he comes too closely upon them. Thoreau remembers one cat that was said to have had wings, perhaps resulting from crossbreeding with a flying squirrel. Although he never sees this cat, he was given a pair of her "wings" (pieces of matted fur that she shed in the springtime), and says that as a poet, he fancies owning a winged cat. Out on the pond in his boat, Thoreau at times pursues the loon, hoping to get close enough for a long look. In general, the loon allows him to advance to only a modest distance before diving deep into the water, surfacing again with a loud laugh. Thoreau sees no rhyme or reason in this ritual, or in the movements of the ducks, or in any of the motions that his other "brute neighbors" go through. He concludes that they must be as enthralled by the water and its natural surroundings as he is.

Summary: House-Warming

Combing the meadows for wild apples and chestnuts, Thoreau is dismayed by how nature's bounty has been plundered for commercial use. Still, there is enough left for him to feast on. The changing leaves of autumn provide a brilliant spectacle, though Thoreau is well aware that they herald the coming hardships of winter. Wasps flee the colder weather in thousands, and Thoreau is forced to retreat to his quarters. He goes to another side of the pond for a while to soak in the remaining rays of the fall sun, which he prefers to "artificial" fire. Toward the end of summer, Thoreau studies masonry to build a chimney for his cabin with the help of his friend Channing. By November, Thoreau's summer labors have proven a good investment, as the fires keep him warm at night.

Walden Pond has begun to freeze over in places, allowing Thoreau to walk on the thin surface and glimpse the deep waters beneath. Fascinating as the underwater activity is, the ice itself equally captivates Thoreau, especially the air bubbles that rise to the surface and wriggle themselves into the ice. Breaking off portions of the ice to examine them and observing the same spots day after day, Thoreau learns how ice forms around the bubbles. He understands how the bubbles make the ice "crack and whoop." With winter fully upon him, Thoreau settles into a winter routine, gathering wood for his fires, and listening to the geese as they migrate south. The gathering of firewood becomes an essential occupation. Thoreau uses various types of wood and brush to kindle his fires, preferring pine but often settling for dry leaves. Warming himself and cooking his food, snugly ensconced with the moles that nest in his cellar, Thoreau reflects that fire warms the poor and the privileged alike, and that every man would die if another ice age occurred.

ANALYSIS

At first glance Thoreau's allegorical dialogue between the hermit and the poet seems fanciful, not very profound, and not well integrated with the animal theme of the chapter. But in fact it reveals much about Thoreau's self-image, and about how he sees his own project not as that of a dreamy artist, but of someone who lives life to its fullest—like the animals before him. The poet in the dialogue offers his silly impressions about how the clouds hang in the sky, and how he has seen nothing like it in old paintings or foreign lands, not even on the coast of Spain. By contrast, the hermit Thoreau's thoughts tend toward more practical concerns like the tubs that need to be scoured, the boiled beef to be eaten, and the fact that his "brown bread will soon be gone." Food is a prominent presence in his meditations, and there is a deep significance in the poet's final complaint that he has not caught enough fish, having used worms that are too large. Thoreau may be hinting that, instead of rhapsodizing about Spain and old pictures, the dreamy poet should have been paying attention to practical matters like the proper bait for fishing. He implies that life is not a poem but a matter of food gathering and survival, and the high-flying artist who ignores this fact will suffer later.

This odd dialogue thus provides a preface to the chapter on animals, "Brute Neighbors," in ironically suggesting that humans and animals are indeed neighbors, and we are all "brutes" seeking food, shelter, and survival. The various vignettes of animal life offered in this chapter focus on animals involved in practical matters of survival, especially in the search for food. The mouse that Thoreau shares his house with is tame and entertaining, but the end point of the entertainment is the acquisition of the bit of cheese. Just like the fishing conversation between the poet and hermit, this interaction between human and mouse is based on food, and it is over when the cheese is gobbled up. The raccoon too is no more truly wild than this half-tamed, home-dwelling mouse. It is not a wild denizen of the forest, but a frequenter of neighborhoods in search of food from human sources. As with the mouse, the animal and human neighbors coexist on the basis of their shared food supplies, which makes feeding the common denominator between them. Similarly, the wild cat that hisses at Thoreau on a walk in the woods was originally, he conjectures, no different from the domestic pet "which has lain on a rug all her days." The housebound and the savage, like the human and the brute, are close counterparts.

The warring ants that Thoreau finds make the connection between humans and brutes no less clear: the distinction between human civilization and animal savagery breaks down when red ants are seen waging a very human war against the black ants. "For numbers and for carnage it was an Austerlitz or a Dresden," says Thoreau, mentioning two famously bloody battles of the nineteenth century. He sees the human aspect of their war immediately. When he narrates the thrilling scene of the large black ant beheading several smaller red ones, we feel the importance of survival even more sharply than we do in the context of food supplies: all these ants are fighting for their lives. The analogy to the human will to survive is clear.

Emphasizing the survival instincts that humans and brutes share does not necessarily imply, for Thoreau, that life is a dead-set fixation on practical gains alone. Animal life, no less than human life, has its eccentricities and irrationalities as part of the package of existence— as Thoreau illustrates by concluding his animal survey with a famously silly creature, the loon. This bird is no less committed to survival than the partridge, the robin, or any of the other birds or beasts mentioned in this chapter. But the loon is also, quite openly, loony. His battle of wits with Thoreau on the pond, diving in a way that makes Thoreau miscalculate where he will reappear and then surfacing unexpectedly elsewhere, serves no practical purpose. He even leads Thoreau to a wider expanse of water where he can maneuver more freely, for no other reason than to increase his fun.

Yet even this game is not played too seriously; the loon puzzles Thoreau by trying hard to sneak up on him only to reveal its location at the last moment. The bird betrays itself because it can afford to do so, since at this moment its life and survival are not at stake. Survival may be the main focus of animal and human existence, but life is more than a struggle, and even nature has its moments of fun and frivolity—like the poet at the beginning. Perhaps the poet and the hermit are not so different, but are rather two aspects of nature and of the man Thoreau imagines himself to be. It is significant that when recounting the old wives' tale about a winged cat, Thoreau says that this "would be the kind of cat for me to keep," since a poet deserves a fantastic animal. This comment is revealing, since with it Thoreau directly acknowledges himself to be a poet, after mocking poets in the opening dialogue. What the chapter shows above all is that, for humans and brutes alike, survival and frivolity are both parts of life.

FORMER INHABITANTS;
AND WINTER VISITORS,
WINTER ANIMALS,
AND THE POND IN WINTER

SUMMARY: FORMER INHABITANTS;
AND WINTER VISITORS

Thoreau spends many winter evenings alone beside his fire, while the snow whirls violently outside his house. He is able to dig a path to town through the deep snow, but has few visitors to his neck of the woods in this cold season. Alone in the wilderness, Thoreau finds himself compelled to conjure up images of those who had endured the hard Walden winters before him.

Although the route between Concord and Lincoln is sparsely populated, Thoreau believes it had been settled more thickly earlier in the century. Many of the earlier inhabitants had been blacks: Thoreau summons up images of Cato Ingraham, the spinster Zilpha, Brister Freeman and his wife, Fenda. Some of their abodes have almost completely vanished, destroyed by age or fire. Thoreau recalls how Breed's hut burned to the ground in a fire twelve years before. Thoreau and the local fire brigade had rushed out to save it, but had found it too far gone. Thoreau recalls seeing the heir to the house lying in shock, muttering to himself about the loss of his property. Near Lincoln, a potter named Wyman had once squatted, followed by his descendants. Another memorable recent inhabitant of the woods was an Irishman named Hugh Quoil, formerly a soldier at the Battle of Waterloo, who had come to live at the Wyman place. All these old-timers are now gone, and Thoreau lives alone amid the ravaged foundations and empty cellar holes that once marked their homes. The site of a once burgeoning village is, by Thoreau's time, marked only by decay, and by grasses and lilacs planted in more prosperous times and outliving their planters. Thoreau muses on the insignificance and transience of humankind's place in nature.

Thoreau has sparse contact with other humans in the depths of winter, and even animals keep to themselves at times. Among Thoreau's most reliable companions are the barred owl, an occasional woodchopper, and his friends William Ellery Channing and the philosopher Amos Bronson Alcott. Thoreau's mentor and benefactor, Ralph Waldo Emerson, also comes. None of these men is directly named in the text, however. Emerson is identified as the "Old Immortal." Thoreau keeps regular watch for "the Visitor who never comes," conforming to an ancient Hindu law of hospitality.

Summary: Winter Animals

Walking over a frozen pond, Thoreau finds everything more open and spacious, with wide yards for sliding and skating on the frozen surface. On these days, the air is filled with the call of the hoot owl and the cry of the goose resounding through the woods. In the morning the red squirrels scuttle and scavenge, at dusk the rabbits come for their feedings, and on moonlit nights the foxes search the snow for prey. Such sounds come and go, but the sounds of snow falling and ice cracking continue through the day and the night. Thoreau places the harvest's unripe corn at his doorstep, attracting smaller squirrels and rabbits to feed near his dwelling. Sometimes he sits and watches the little creatures paw at their food for hours. At other times they carry their bounty away into the forest, discarding their refuse in various spots. This refuse attracts the jays, chickadees, and sparrows that descend upon the leftover cobs and pick at them. On certain mornings and afternoons, Thoreau hears hounds yelping in pursuit of their quarry. Thoreau often talks with the huntsmen who pass by Walden.

Summary: The Pond in Winter

Thoreau's first task on waking up is to collect water for the day. In the winter this job proves difficult, as he has to chop through the ice. He is soon joined by a hardy group of fisherman. Thoreau is amused by their primitive methods, but is more amazed by what they catch, notably the distinctively colored pickerel, which stands out from the more typically celebrated cod and haddock of the sea.

In an effort to measure the depth of Walden Pond and dispel the myth that it is bottomless, Thoreau uses a fishing line and a light stone. Many locals believe the pond to be bottomless, but Thoreau measures it at just over one hundred feet. Thoreau meditates on the way people wish to believe in a symbol of heaven and infinity. Through repeated soundings, Thoreau is able to get a general sense of the shape of Walden Pond's bottom, and learns that it conforms to the surrounding terrain. The pond reaches its greatest depth at the point of its greatest length and breadth. Thoreau wonders if this might be a clue to pinpointing the deepest points of larger bodies of water, such as oceans. To test this hypothesis, Thoreau plumbs the nearby White Pond. Again, the point of greatest depth is quite near to the point where the axis of greatest length intersects the axis of greatest breadth. Having more evidence to bolster his theory, Thoreau extends it to a metaphorical level, supposing that a person's behavior and circumstances will determine the depths of his or her soul.

In Thoreau's second winter at the pond, a team of one hundred men and more arrives at Walden Pond. Acting as agents for an ambitious farmer, these workmen cut and cut at the ice over a period of two weeks, claiming they could harvest as much as a thousand tons on a good day and ten thousand tons over the whole winter. It is a complex business, on a grand scale, and the result is a great heap of ice to be stored and later sold for a profit. Although some of it reaches far-off destinations, Thoreau notes that the greater part of it melts and returns to the pond.

ANALYSIS: FORMER INHABITANTS; AND WINTER VISITORS, WINTER ANIMALS, AND THE POND IN WINTER

These three chapters are dominated by winter, a time for stepping back from outside work and withdrawing to the inner world of home and mind. As a result, this portion of *Walden* is brooding and highly meditative, focusing on ideas of absence, history, and infinity. "Former Inhabitants; and Winter Visitors " is a survey of Walden's ghosts, or at least of earlier residents of the pond who are "conjured up," as Thoreau says, in his own mind. Prominent among the dead he conjures up from the graves of history are black people: Cato Ingraham, Zilpha, and Brister Freeman are all poor blacks who are alive no longer, but still live in Thoreau's personal memory. Given Thoreau's strong opposition to Southern slavery and his proven commitment to aiding fugitive slaves, his reminiscences of black people here take on an ideological importance. We sense that Thoreau is recalling them because the nation's official chronicles do not: in a generally racist country, individuals must provide a humane commemoration for those who are otherwise overlooked and forgotten.

The absent black people segue in Thoreau's imagination to another absence: that of the hut that had once belonged to Breed before it burned down a dozen years earlier. This story of a mere house takes on a symbolic meaning. As Thoreau narrates the story of how he and the other local fire volunteer firefighters rushed to save the hut, only to decide "to let it burn, it was so far gone and so worthless," our thoughts turn to the inevitable end to all things, houses and people alike. The moral is that it is useless to struggle to preserve them, for destruction will come regardless of our efforts. Thoreau says of the deceased Irishman, Hugh Quoil, that "[a]ll I know of him is tragic," and the same could be said of almost everything he mentions in these wintry and death-obsessed chapters. His focus on the mortality of all life has a biblical feeling, as in the theme of *memento mori* (Latin for "remember you shall die") common in New England Protestant sermons and prayer books. When Thoreau mentions scripture in this chapter, his words sound even more religious. The theological opposite of all this mortality is, of course, immortal heaven. Thoreau again equates heaven on earth with water, like that of Walden Pond or Breed's well, "which, thank Heaven, could never be burned." Water is the only thing impervious to the fires of death, and so there are spots of immortality even amid these ruins of destruction. When Thoreau later dubs his occasional visitor Emerson an "Old Immortal," we feel that philosophy is another such spot, and that the water's eternity is connected to the eternal truths glimpsed by great minds.

The idea of eternity is deeply sounded in the chapter "The Pond in Winter," which focuses on the question of whether Walden Pond is, as people rumor it to be, infinite. Thoreau is determined to measure its depths, just as he reaches into the depths of himself in his backwoods retirement. The newly fallen snow makes the pond hard to locate, and the result is suggestive: the purity within us could be anywhere, if we can pierce the surface of our earthly lives. When Thoreau finds Walden Pond, cuts through the icy layer on top, and gazes into the "perennial waveless serenity" within, his conclusions are theological rather than natural, or both at once. "Heaven," he says, "is under our feet as well as over our heads." Thoreau seems satisfied that the pond should be seen as a bottomless quantity of water descending all the way to the other side of the globe, since it encourages inspirational thoughts of infinity.

We might infer that some men, like Thoreau, do not need symbols of infinity, since they experience infinity directly: the infinity of man's spirit. Thoreau is content to prove that Walden Pond is only a hundred feet deep, since he knows that real depth is elsewhere, in his own mind and soul. Thoreau compares ice and water to the intellect and the emotions respectively, thus depicting the entire human spirit as composed of different aqueous states: the human *is* water. He sees a reflection of himself in the cut ice, "a double shadow of myself," mirrored in the water. Thus every time he goes for a drink of water, he communes with the timeless aspect of his own self. Water becomes a metaphor not just for heaven but also, more important, for the human soul that is itself heavenly, for the divine side of humankind. This divinity can never be depleted, as Thoreau hints in his detailed account of ice cutting, which in the winter of 1846 yields ten thousand tons—most of which melts and flows back ultimately to the pond again, so that "the pond recovered the greater part." It is the living source, inexhaustible.

SPRING AND CONCLUSION

SUMMARY: SPRING

With the coming of April, the ice begins to melt from Walden Pond, creating a thunderous roar in which Thoreau delights. Thoreau mentions an old man he knows—whose wisdom, Thoreau says, he could not rival if he lived to be as old as Methuselah—who was struck with terror by the crash of the melting ice despite his long experience with the ways of nature. Thoreau describes it as a kind of universal meltdown, heralding total change. The sand moves with the flowing rivulets of water. Buds and leaves appear. Wild geese fly overhead, trumpeting through the heavens. Thoreau feels that old grudges should be abandoned and old sins forgiven in this time of renewed life. Inspired by the arrival of good weather, Thoreau takes to fishing again. He admires a graceful, solitary hawk circling overhead. He senses the throb of universal life and spiritual upheaval, and meditates that death in such an atmosphere can have no sting. His mission completed, Thoreau leaves Walden Pond on September 6, 1847.

Summary: Conclusion

> *It is not worth the while to go round the world to*
> *count the cats in Zanzibar.*   (See QUOTATIONS, p. 65)

Thoreau notes that doctors often recommend a change of scenery for the sick, but he slyly mocks this view, saying that the "universe is wider than our views of it." He argues that it is perhaps a change of soul, rather than a change of landscape, that is needed. Thoreau remarks that his reasons for leaving Walden Pond are as good as his reasons for going: he has other lives to live, and has changes to experience. He says that anyone confidently attempting to live "in the direction of his dreams" will meet with uncommon success, and calls this dream life the real destination that matters, not going off "to count the cats in Zanzibar." He laments the downgraded sensibility and cheapened lives of contemporary Americans, wondering why his countrymen are in such a desperate hurry to succeed. He urges us to sell our fancy clothes and keep our thoughts, get rid of our civilized shells and find our truer selves. Life near the bone, says Thoreau, "is sweetest." Superfluous wealth can buy superfluities only, and "[m]oney is not required to buy one necessary of the soul." He reflects on the dinner parties taking place in the city, the amusing anecdotes about California and Texas, and compares it all to a swamp where one must seek the rock bottom by oneself. Thoreau reflects that we humans do not know where we are and that we are asleep half the time. This puny existence leads him to describe himself as "me the human insect," and to meditate on the "greater Benefactor and Intelligence" that stands over him.

Thoreau concludes by acknowledging that the average "John or Jonathon" reading his words will not understand them, but that this does not matter. A new day is dawning, and the sun "is a morning star" heralding a new life to come.

Analysis

The biblical references slipped into Thoreau's nature writing throughout the work become more marked in the final chapters of *Walden*. The Old Testament figure of Methuselah is mentioned, and there are clear evocations of the creation story of Genesis in Thoreau's comparison of man to clay: "What is man but a mass of thawing clay?" God the creator is mentioned several times in "Spring," as when he is described as having patented a leaf, or when Thoreau depicts the green world as the laboratory of "the Artist who made the world and me." More pagan, but equally powerful as myth, is Thoreau's similar reference to spring as being "like the creation of Cosmos out of Chaos and the realization of the Golden Age." This description alludes to the ancient Greek notion that the gods brought order to the cosmos, thereby creating the analogue of Christian paradise—the Golden Age. Here again, every human in springtime seems to become Adam or Eve before the Fall, full of infinite potential. These theological references give a deep symbolic meaning, though always subtle and understated, to the revitalization of nature that occurs in this chapter. It is more than a change in the climate. The coming of spring brings not just warmer weather to Walden Pond, but also an allegorical renewal of life, a spiritual rebirth. The long, detailed description of the melting ice, transformed from stasis to movement and fluidity, suggests the freedom promised by the living water of Christian baptism. This thaw marks the end of the story, just as Thoreau chooses to make spring the end of his own work, rather than, as might be expected, the beginning. By ending his account in the spring, Thoreau points us toward the open future and the unlived potential of our own lives.

Also occupying a final position in Christian Scripture is the Apocalypse described in the Book of Revelations, the last book of the Bible, which also promises a transformed future for our own lives. There are strong apocalyptic images in Thoreau's "Spring." The roar of the shaken earth on Judgment Day is echoed in the strange and wild sound of the breaking ice heard by the old man described by Thoreau. That the old man, who Thoreau says knows all of nature's operations, has never encountered this sound before gives us the feeling that this wild roar is more supernatural and heavenly. Similarly, the great heavenly armies of the Apocalypse are hinted at by the wild geese called "into rank" by "their commander," flying overhead with a thunderous flapping. The wild honk of the head goose evokes the angel's trumpet blare that, according to the Bible, will herald the onset of Judgment Day. The earth, as Thoreau describes it, is transfigured into a higher form of existence, and life becomes celestial. Thoreau has a vision of gold and jewels reminiscent of the divine riches described in Revelations, no less valuable in actually being the fish he has caught. This wealth is not earthly but rather seems heaven-sent, as it is in the Apocalypse. In all these images of majesty and heaven, Thoreau blends

nature writing and religious writing, creating his own religion of a new life to come, an imminent springtime for the individual soul.

Thoreau's relationship with us becomes more intense, even passionate, in these final chapters. The easygoing description and anecdotal storytelling of earlier chapters gives way here to a more urgent tone, almost at times sermonizing. There are far more direct commands than ever before: Thoreau tells us to "[s]ell your clothes and keep your thoughts," and "[s]ay what you have to say, not what you ought." These are not religious injunctions, but still there is a feeling that Thoreau is in the pulpit and we are in the church pew, receiving his words as moral instruction. But his stern orders to "you" do not imply superiority in his own position, as if he is talking down to us. Generally he includes himself in his own dictates, referring to "us" and thereby including himself. This rhetoric is different from ordering us to obey the truth: it implies that he is subject to the same higher laws that we are, and susceptible to the same temptations and risks. It is a morally righteous tone, but it is also egalitarian, resonating with a conviction that we are all humans together. This hint of American equality is heard in his command to accept poverty or riches without concern: "Love your life, poor as it is." The rich may not love their lives any better than the poor: all are equal. At times there is even a direct echo of American rhetoric in Thoreau's words, as when he says, "Rather than love, than money, than fame, give me truth," echoing the American revolutionary slogan, "Give me liberty or give me death." In these intense and intimate addresses to us that emerge at the end of the work, replacing the meandering rhythms of the first chapter, we sense the urgency of Thoreau's final message to us. The work he has written is meant to mobilize us to start working to live our lives differently.

SUMMARY & ANALYSIS

IMPORTANT QUOTATIONS EXPLAINED

1. The mass of men lead lives of quiet desperation.

This sentence, which appears in the first chapter, "Economy," is perhaps the most famous quotation from *Walden*. It sums up the prophetic side of Thoreau that many people forget about; he was not just an experimenter living in isolation on Walden Pond, but also a deeply social and morally inspired writer with an ardent message for the masses. His use of the word "desperation" instead of a milder reference to discontentment or unhappiness shows the grimness of his vision of the mainstream American lifestyle. He believes that the monomaniacal pursuit of success and wealth has paradoxically cheapened the lives of those engaged in it, making them unable to appreciate the simpler pleasures enumerated in *Walden*. But the unpleasantness of American life, according to Thoreau, is more than simply financial or economic, despite the title of his first chapter. "Desperation" is also a word with deep religious connotations, the "lack of hope" that, according to Dante (one of Thoreau's favorite writers), was inscribed on the gates at hell's entrance. *The Pilgrim's Progress,* John Bunyan's Protestant spiritual classic and a bestseller in the New England of Thoreau's day, features a hero who passes through a bleak lowland called the Slough of Despair on his way to meet God. By asserting that most humans have gotten stuck in despair, Thoreau is implying that they are unable to continue farther on their pilgrimage toward true redemption.

2. So that all the pecuniary outgoes, excepting for
washing and mending, which for the most part were
done out of the house, and their bills have not yet
been received . . . were

House,	$28 12 ½
Farm one year,	14 72 ½
Food eight months,	8 74
Clothing &c., eight months,	8 40 ¾
Oil, &c., eight months,	2 00
In all,	$61 99 ¾

One of several bookkeeping excerpts included in *Walden,* this one from the chapter "Economy" shows that, as the chapter's title indicates, Thoreau is not a free spirit fleeing social realities, but on the contrary has a businessman's sharp eye for financial matters. Indeed, many first-time readers of *Walden* are surprised to find so much minute financial detail in what they expect to be inspirational nature writing. But this is Thoreau's point: the true inspiration of the spirit does not need to entail financial failure or misery, and economic and spiritual well-being are two sides of the same coin. Since money is a social rather than a natural phenomenon, we see the complexity of Thoreau's turn to nature: he is not really escaping the world of human values at all, but rather extending it. He defines his success in his Walden project not solely in terms of his own spiritual development but also in economic terms—he seeks to live without incurring debt. Money defines his freedom as much as spiritual transcendence does.

Nonetheless, Thoreau's account-keeping also reveals the amateur nature of his project, and feeds our underlying knowledge that he is a Harvard man slumming temporarily in the woods rather than a truly needy person struggling to make ends meet. Any accountant would be quick to point out Thoreau's failure to include his laundry bills in his grand total, on the frivolous grounds that they have not come in yet. He inconsistently lists a year's rent on the farm, but only eight months' expenditures on food and clothing. If he were truly in need, he might be forced to keep better books; we sense that his accounting, like much of *Walden* in general, is visionary fantasy in the guise of fact.

3. I went to the woods because I wished to live
    deliberately, to front only the essential facts of life,
    and see if I could not learn what it had to teach, and
    not, when I came to die, discover that I had not lived.

These words provide the answer to the question posed by the title of Thoreau's chapter "Where I Lived, and What I Lived For." The first part of this title is a practical concern about a place of residence, while the second part is a deeply philosophical concern about the meaning of life. Thoreau combines the practical and the philosophical in his Walden project, and thus the phrase "the essential facts of life" can refer both to material necessities like food and shelter and also to the core of human existence. The double aspect of *Walden,* its treatment of hard facts as well as philosophical questions, is also evident in his mention of living at the end. Taken factually and literally, it is of course impossible for Thoreau to die understanding that "I had not lived." But taken philosophically, life means not just biological functioning but also inner fulfillment. The experimentalism of Thoreau's endeavor is expressed in his frank acknowledgement that he is testing out an idea, rather than proving a foregone conclusion. Finally, the obscure mystical side of Thoreau—which makes him often appear more of a visionary than a philosopher—is evident in his famous phrase "to live deliberately." On a literal level, he wishes to choose his path of life independently and thoughtfully, subject to his own deliberation and no one else's. But on a higher level, the phrase is mystical and haunting, since of course nobody ever *chooses* to live or deliberately seeks to exist. As elsewhere in the work, Thoreau here forces us to contemplate the transcendent meaning of human life even while we think he is simply referring to a cabin in the woods.

QUOTATIONS

4.   A field of water betrays the spirit that is in the air. It is
     continually receiving new life and motion from above.
     It is intermediate between land and sky.

This description of Walden Pond from the chapter entitled "The
Ponds" shows how insufficient the label "nature writer" is when
applied to the mystical vision of Thoreau when he regards the landscape around him. It is true that he describes the flora and fauna of
Concord with a level of vibrancy and specificity to which nature
writers aspire, but he does more than merely observe and take notes.
He also, at times, transforms the physical environment into a spiritual vision, with religious rather than practical or scientific meaning. Here the phrase "the spirit that is in the air" is more reminiscent
of a preacher or poet than a naturalist. It is hard scientifically to
define what exactly the "new life" is that comes to the water from
the sky, but in a transcendental, intuitive, spiritual context it makes
perfect sense. Even the description of the pond as an "intermediate
between land and sky" has more of an allegorical meaning than a
physical one, since in physical terms the pond is not *between* land
and sky at all. Allegorically, the pond is the human soul at the junc-
ture between earth and heaven, living in an earthly realm but reflecting a peaceful world above just as the pond reflects the sky. Thoreau
makes this parallel almost explicit when he compares the depth of
the pond to the depth of the soul.

5.   It is not worth the while to go round the world to count the cats in Zanzibar.

This statement from the "Conclusion" of *Walden* illustrates another debt on Thoreau's part to the American Transcendentalist school of his philosophical mentor, Ralph Waldo Emerson. In Emerson's influential essay "Self-Reliance," which Thoreau's Walden project could be said to put into practice, Emerson makes the assertion that "travel is a fool's paradise," and that it is far more useful to change one's soul than to change one's landscape. The fool who thinks that his life will change on a trip to Europe is shocked and disappointed to discover, after unpacking his suitcase on arrival, that he is still in the same tedious company of himself. For Emerson the futility of travel is simply a consequence of his belief in the centrality of the self—the depth and health of the soul—in all human affairs. Thoreau inherits this same belief, downgrading the usual glamour of international travel (in this case to Zanzibar, off the coast of East Africa) with the ridiculous enterprise of counting felines. The point of this mockery is to point to a better alternative to African voyages. As he intimates earlier when he ironically notes that he has traveled a lot in Concord, Thoreau insists that the most valuable kind of travel occurs without leaving one's hometown: the inward voyage of soul-searching.

KEY FACTS

FULL TITLE
Originally published as *Walden; or, Life in the Woods.* Thoreau
requested that the title be abbreviated simply to *Walden* upon
the preparation of a second edition in 1862.

AUTHOR
Henry David Thoreau

TYPE OF WORK
Essay

GENRE
Autobiography; moral philosophy; natural history;
social criticism

LANGUAGE
English

TIME AND PLACE WRITTEN
1845–1854, Walden Pond, near Concord, Massachusetts

DATE OF FIRST PUBLICATION
1854

PUBLISHER
Ticknor and Fields, Boston

NARRATOR
Henry David Thoreau

POINT OF VIEW
Thoreau narrates in the first person, using the word "I" nearly
2,000 times in the narrative of Walden. Defending this
approach, he remarks, "I should not talk so much about myself
if there were any body else whom I knew as well."

TONE
Thoreau's tone varies throughout the work. In some places he is
mystical and lyrical, as in the blue ice description in "Ponds."
He can be hardheaded and practical, as in the accounting details
of "Economy." Sometimes he seems to be writing a diary,
recording the day's events; other times he widens his scope to

include the whole cosmos and all eternity. In some places his style is neutral and observational, in other places powerfully prophetic or didactic, as in the chapter "Conclusion."

TENSE
Thoreau uses the past tense for recounting his Walden experiments and the present tense for the more meditative and philosophical passages.

SETTING (TIME)
Summer 1845 through Summer 1847 (although the book condenses the two years into one)

SETTING (PLACE)
Walden Pond

PROTAGONIST
Henry David Thoreau

MAJOR CONFLICT
Thoreau resists the constraints of civilized American life.

RISING ACTION
Thoreau builds a small dwelling by Walden Pond and moves to the wilderness.

CLIMAX
Thoreau endures the winter and feels spring's transforming power arrive.

FALLING ACTION
Thoreau, accustomed to a solitary life in the woods, concludes his project and moves back to Concord and social existence.

THEMES
The importance of self-reliance; the value of simplicity; the illusion of progress

MOTIFS
The seasonal cycle; poetry; imaginary people

SYMBOLS
Animals; ice; Walden Pond

FORESHADOWING
Thoreau tells us in the first paragraph of the work that he has left Walden Pond, foreshadowing the exit he narrates at the end.

Study Questions & Essay Topics

Study Questions

1. *In a speech from the early 1940s, the poet Ezra Pound dismissed Thoreau's project in less than twenty-five words. Pound viewed it as Thoreau's:*

   > First intellectual reaction to mere approach of industrialization: Thoreau tried to see how little he need bother about other humanity.

   Would you agree with Pound that the experiment Thoreau takes up at Walden Pond demonstrates his indifference to other humans? Why or why not?

While Thoreau clearly voices some sharp criticism of civilized life and industrialization, Pound is wrong in claiming that Thoreau does not care about "other humanity" at all. Thoreau's retreat to Walden Pond is never framed as an attempt to flee humans, and he explicitly points out that he visits Concord several times a week, that he enjoys entertaining visitors in his shack, and that he has had more guests at the pond than ever before. His friendly chats with the Canadian woodcutter Alex Therien show his sociability, and his domestic management lectures to John Field and Field's family, though they may be undiplomatic, come from Thoreau's very committed desire to pull him out of poverty. He never shows any signs of indifference to humanity. On the contrary, his prophetic tone at the end of the work displays a huge moral investment in the fate of his fellow men.

2.   *Does Thoreau show socialist tendencies, though he is
     writing before socialism is a recognized idea?*

Certainly Thoreau's call to "simplify, simplify, simplify" our lives
contradicts the spirit of American conspicuous consumption and
modern capitalism. Thoreau would prefer us to patch our old
clothes instead of buying new ones, disdaining the latest fashions
dictated to us by advertisers and department stores. He would have
us eat rice on our front porch instead of going to fine restaurants,
and he would prefer to see us quit our well-paid jobs in order to pursue our more rewarding development as humans. This rejection of
economic success, high social rank, and consumerism is typical of
the broad current of socialist thought that emerged later in the nineteenth century. But in other respects, Thoreau is no true socialist. He
shows little solidarity with the poor and underprivileged: though he
sometimes stops to chat with them, he never lets us forget that he is
better educated and more advanced than they, as when he refers to
Therien's "animal nature." A socialist must identify with the masses
of workers, but Thoreau is a stubborn individualist. Moreover, he
underestimates the power of social circumstances (such as discrimination against immigrants) in creating poverty, as we clearly see
when he blames John Field's poverty on his being Irish. He is not
really an analyst of the wealth of nations, but more of a prophet
who uses economics as an allegory for self-reliance and spiritual
well being.

3.   *Thoreau makes it very clear at the opening of Walden that
     his stay in the wilderness was not a lifestyle choice but
     rather a temporary experiment, and that "At present I am
     a sojourner in civilized life again." Does the short
     duration of Thoreau's stay at Walden undercut the
     importance of his project?*

One widespread misunderstanding of Thoreau is that he was a critic of modernity who failed in his plan to live a more authentic life on his own. But, in fact, Thoreau insists on telling us that his Walden project is not a life decision or a commitment to a set of ideals, but an experiment in alternative living that is unambiguously amateurish. It is more like casual play than like solemn ideology. This informality explains why, when he leaves Walden Pond in 1847, Thoreau does not admit failure; rather, he says simply that he has other lives to live. Thoreau was more of an Emersonian transcendentalist than he was a socialist: the soul mattered more to him than sociology. He was not as interested in being a model farmer as in showing how the soul could benefit from a change of scenery and occupation. Having learned the lessons that Walden Pond had to offer him, he turned to other scenes and other occupations, thus proving rather than undercutting his philosophy of life.

SUGGESTED ESSAY TOPICS

1.   Thoreau occasionally forces a long series of tedious details upon us, as for example when in "House-Warming" he tells us a precise history of the freezing of Walden Pond over the past several years. Similarly detailed passages refer to his farming endeavors, his home construction, and other topics. Why does Thoreau repeatedly display these irrelevant details? How do they fit in to his overall plan for *Walden*?

2.   Thoreau has inspired twentieth-century leaders such as Martin Luther King and Mahatma Gandhi, but it is not certain that he had any leadership potential himself, though he often posed as a kind of prophet for his fellowman. Is Thoreau a leader? Why or why not? 3. At times Thoreau seems like a diarist narrating the flow of everyday events, as humdrum as they may be. At other times he is almost a mystic writer, as when he compares the topography of ponds to the shape of the human soul. And at still other times he is a social critic and moral prophet. Does the hodgepodge of genres in *Walden* contribute something positive to its overall meaning for us?

4.   Thoreau is a practical man and a close observer of nature, but he is also a fantasist who makes a lot of references to mythology. In "Economy" he mentions the Greek myth of Deucalion and Pyrrha who created men by throwing stones over their shoulders; in "The Pond in Winter" he compares a pile of ice to Valhalla, palace of the Scandinavian gods. In "Sounds" he describes the Fitchburg Railway train as a great mythical beast invading the calm of Walden. What is the effect of all these mythological references? Do they change the overall message of the work in any important way?

QUESTIONS & ESSAYS

5. Thoreau repeatedly praises the simplicity and industriousness of the working poor, and comes very close to joining their ranks when he lives at subsistence level in the woods for two years. Yet in his chapter on reading he disdains popular tastes in books, implying that everyone should be able to read the Greek tragedian Aeschylus in the original, as he does. His allusions to world literature are quite lofty, including Chinese philosophers and Persian poets. Is Thoreau a snob? If so, is his democratic populism undermined by his disdain for popular culture?

6. What would Thoreau make of the fact that *Walden* is one of the most commonly assigned texts in high school and college literature courses across the country? Would he welcome the fact that he has become part of the mainstream culture that he was criticizing?

Review & Resources

Quiz

1. What, in the chapter "Sounds," does Thoreau describe as having the roar of a fierce beast?

    A. A wolf
    B. A moose
    C. A train
    D. A riverboat

2. In what town did Thoreau spend most of his life?

    A. Boston
    B. Concord
    C. Plymouth
    D. Providence

3. What college did Thoreau attend?

    A. Amherst
    B. Harvard
    C. Oxford
    D. Yale

4. In what season does Thoreau conclude his stay at Walden Pond?

    A. Summer
    B. Winter
    C. Autumn
    D. Spring

5. When did Thoreau move in to his house at Walden Pond?

    A. 1836
    B. 1845
    C. 1848
    D. 1854

6. What, according to Thoreau, do the mass of men lead?

    A.   Lives of quiet deprecation
    B.   Lives of quiet derivation
    C.   Lives of quiet desperation
    D.   Lives of quiet deviation

7. Which of the following was closest to Thoreau's house at Walden Pond?

    A.   A canal
    B.   A mill
    C.   A railroad
    D.   A school

8. What was the approximate maximum number of visitors that Thoreau received in his house at a single time?

    A.   One
    B.   Three
    C.   Thirteen
    D.   Thirty

9. Which crop did Thoreau raise in the greatest quantity?

    A.   Beans
    B.   Peas
    C.   Potatoes
    D.   Turnips

10. What war was the United States involved in during Thoreau's stay at Walden Pond?

    A.   The Civil War
    B.   The French and Indian War
    C.   The Mexican War
    D.   The Spanish-American War

11. For what was Thoreau put into jail by the town constable?

    A.   Perjury
    B.   Tax evasion
    C.   Treason
    D.   Trespass

12. Which of the following is not the name of a pond
    Thoreau describes?

    A. Flints' Pond
    B. Golden Pond
    C. Goose Pond
    D. White Pond

13. When Thoreau encounters a woodchuck in the woods, how
    does he react?

    A. He wants to paint a picture of it
    B. He wants to speak with it
    C. He wants to capture it and keep it for his pet
    D. He wants to eat it

14. Which poet made frequent visits to Thoreau's cabin
    at Walden?

    A. William Ellery Channing
    B. Emily Dickinson
    C. Walt Whitman
    D. William Wordsworth

15. Between what creatures does Thoreau witness a battle?

    A. Ants
    B. Mice
    C. Birds
    D. Cats

16. Which philosopher pays a lengthy visit to Thoreau's cabin
    at Walden?

    A. Amos Bronson Alcott
    B. George Santayana
    C. John Dewey
    D. William James

REVIEW & RESOURCES

17. To what does Thoreau partly attribute John Field's poverty?

   A. His physical handicaps
   B. His small farm
   C. Unfair discrimination by local employers
   D. His Irish heritage

18. Approximately how deep is Walden Pond at its deepest point?

   A. 10 feet
   B. 50 feet
   C. 100 feet
   D. 500 feet

19. Why do a large group of men arrive at Walden Pond in the winter of 1846–1847?

   A. To chop down a number of trees
   B. To clear the pond of ice for commercial sale
   C. To play a game of ice hockey
   D. To pressure Thoreau into paying the debts he has accumulated in back-taxes

20. Which of the following does Thoreau value most highly?

   A. Fame
   B. Love
   C. Money
   D. Truth

21. What, as Thoreau describes it at the end of the work, is the sun?

   A. A lantern in the sky
   B. A morning star
   C. A red dwarf waiting to happen
   D. A symbol of our lives

22. What was the title of Thoreau's first published book?

    A. *A Week on the Merrimack and Concord Rivers*
    B. "Civil Disobedience"
    C. *Nature*
    D. *Walden*

23. What cause did Thoreau take up most earnestly in the 1850s?

    A. Abolitionism
    B. Labor Reform
    C. Temperance
    D. Women's Suffrage

24. What is Thoreau's interaction with the loon mentioned at the end of "Brute Neighbors"?

    A. He is imitating it
    B. He is painting it
    C. He is hunting it
    D. He is playing with it

25. What color is the ice of Walden Pond?

    A. Bluish
    B. Yellowish
    C. Pure white
    D. Greenish

SUGGESTION FOR FURTHER READING

BICKMAN, MARTIN. WALDEN: *Volatile Truths.* New York: Twayne, 1992.

BRIDGMAN, RICHARD. *Dark Thoreau.* Lincoln: University of Nebraska Press, 1982.

CAVELL, STANLEY. *The Senses of Walden: An Expanded Edition.* San Francisco: North Point Press, 1981.

EMERSON, RALPH WALDO. *Essays and Lectures.* New York: Library of America, 1983.

HARDING, WALTER, ed. WALDEN: *An Annotated Edition.* New York: Houghton Mifflin, 1995.

JOHNSON, WILLIAM C. *What Thoreau Said:* WALDEN *and the Unsayable.* Moscow, Idaho: University of Idaho Press, 1991.

MYERSON, JOEL, ed. *Critical Essays on Henry David Thoreau's* WALDEN. Boston: G. K. Hall, 1988.

SAYRE, ROBERT F., ed. *New Essays on* WALDEN. Cambridge: Cambridge University Press, 1992.

SPARKNOTES TEST PREPARATION GUIDES

The SparkNotes team figured it was time to cut standardized tests down to size. We've studied the tests for you, so that SparkNotes test prep guides are:

Smarter:
Packed with critical-thinking skills and test-
taking strategies that will improve your score.

Better:
Fully up to date, covering all new features of the tests,
with study tips on every type of question.

Faster:
Our books cover exactly what you need to
know for the test. No more, no less.

SparkNotes Guide to the SAT & PSAT
SparkNotes Guide to the SAT & PSAT—Deluxe Internet Edition
SparkNotes Guide to the ACT
SparkNotes Guide to the ACT—Deluxe Internet Edition
SparkNotes Guide to the SAT II Writing
SparkNotes Guide to the SAT II U.S. History
SparkNotes Guide to the SAT II Math Ic
SparkNotes Guide to the SAT II Math IIc
SparkNotes Guide to the SAT II Biology
SparkNotes Guide to the SAT II Physics

SAT and PSAT are registered trademarks of the College Entrance Examination Board, which does not endorse these books.
ACT is a registered trademark of ACT, Inc. which neither sponsors nor endorses these books.

SparkNotes Study Guides: